Gail Russell
A Biography of an Actress

By K.C. Motsinger

JC Publications
Sacramento, Ca

Gail Russell
A Biography of an Actress

By K.C. Motsinger

(ISBN-13): 978-0692748008
Includes, index, bibliography, and chapter notes.
©2016 Copyright by K.C Motsinger

No part of this book may be reproduced or transmitted in any form or by any means, graphic, electronic, or mechanical, including photocopying, recording, taping or by any information storage retrieval system without the written permission of K.C Motsinger.

Cover design by Williams writing, editing, and design©

Manufactured in the United States

JC Publications
Sacramento, Ca
JCPublication.com

Dedicated to the wide eyed girl who only wanted to paint the wondrous things on Earth and is now painting elsewhere on a different canvas.

"I just wanted to get away from people and paint."

Gail Russell, 1960

Table of Contents

Acknowledgments	5
Preface	6
Foreword	8
Chapter 1	9
Chapter 2	11
Chapter 3	17
Chapter 4	22
Chapter 5	40
Chapter 6	57
Photographs	65
Chapter 7	114
Chapter 8	123
Chapter 9	130
Chapter 10	136
Chapter 11	141
Chapter 12	147
Chapter 13	155
Chapter 14	160
Chapter 15	168
Afterword	172
Gail Russell filmography	173
Bibliography	174
Chapter notes	176
Index	189

Acknowledgments

I wish to thank Jimmy Lydon and Roger Mobley for sharing their memories of Gail Russell. James Curl, who wrote the excellent biography of boxer Jersey Joe Walcott, for his work publishing. Tom Weaver another author, the best interviewer of people that worked in Hollywood's golden age, Ron Stephenson for sharing his vast collection of Gail Russell memorabilia and anecdotes, Charlie Timmons for his help sorting out the family background and supplying numerous photographs of Gail's personal items. His contributions were invaluable. Bridget Madison and Andrew J. Fenady for taking the time to talk to me, Kory Cope on the manuscript, and the local library for answering numerous requests for references.

James Curl discovered that his mother Gail was named after Gail Russell.

Preface

The first movie I ever saw with John Wayne was "Wake of the Red Witch," playing on the afternoon movie on television. I vaguely remember the lady who died during the flashback sequence: Gail Russell. The majority of movies ended with happy endings, but in this film the star and co-star both perished. This created quite a jolt for an eight-year-old seeing a movie with a different type of ending. Later, the film "The Uninvited" played on the late night Saturday night horror movie, but it was so talky and slow that I never waited around for the ending. I was used to the Universal or Hammer films which got to the monster or ghost right away. Kids don't often have lots of patience.

Many years later after growing up, the movie was on and I realized what I missed. The ending was as frightening as ever seen in a movie. At the beginning of the movie the moderator introduced the cast. When Gail Russell's name was mentioned the word "tragic" was used; describing how she battled stage fright, turning to alcohol to get through the film process and passing away at a young age. More of her films were shown and I watched everyone. It was obvious the camera liked her and she came across as a good actress too. Still, I wondered what specifically happened to her.

Checking on the web and library there wasn't a total biography about her; a chapter in one book, bits, and pieces in others. The E! Network telecast a series of documentaries about Hollywood tragedies entitled: "Mysteries and Scandals" including one on Gail Russell. This episode answered most of the questions about her life, but left some room for others. That's when I decided to write a book on Gail Russell.

I knew the story would have a sad ending like her character Angelique in "Wake of the Red Witch." During the course of writing, I experienced several dreams of Gail Russell. In one she was dressed as Angelique sitting in an auditorium. I approached her asking what John Wayne was like. She replied, "Go over and meet him." Wayne was up on stage the image of Captain Ralls. In another dream a scene from the film "The Unseen" took place. I walked into an area. Gail was sitting on a sofa, her character Miss Howard in repose.

The most vivid dream occurred one night. I was sitting outside at a table talking to Gail. The studio bus pulled up to take her to Paramount. She jumped up crying, running away. Gail was sitting outside the studio crying surrounded by other actresses from Paramount trying to comfort her. One actress looked up saying, "Leave her alone!"

If only everyone had done that, Gail Russell might have stayed around a little longer.

K.C Motsinger, 2015

Foreword
The Movie Star we knew as "Aunt Gail"

Gail was about 21-years-old when I was born in Huntington Park, California (West L.A County). I grew up in Bell Gardens, California (L.A County). Gail's mother's (Gladys) sister, Ruth Emma was my grandmother and although we called her "aunt Gail" (probably easier to say) we were actually second cousins. My mother was Mary Stella, (coincidence Gail's character in the "Uninvited" was Stella and her mother, Mary).

The first time I remember seeing Aunt Gail was one Christmas day when her and "Uncle Guy" Madison stopped by the house and gave me a stuffed toy skunk. I was about three-years-old. Every once in a while, everyone would go to my grandmas, Ruth Emma (Gail's Aunt) but I don't think Gail's mom, dad or brother came, just Gail and Guy. Sometimes his co-star in "The Adventures of Wild Bill Hickok" Andy Devine came because he liked my grandmother's chicken. My brother (three years older) commented one time, "boy that guy could eat," and it showed. Andy was a big jovial man with a heart to match.

Now that I look back, I think Gail liked coming over there because there was no pressure and they could relax and enjoy family. Then in the early '50s we moved to Placerville, California; north about 600 miles and we didn't see much of them. Except for one time Gail and Guy came by and gave my dad an autographed "Guy Madison" felt cowboy hat. My dad about wore that hat out!

I think Gail wanted kids but couldn't. We all liked Guy. Next thing I know my mom, aunt and I were headed south for Gail's funeral. I was about 16-years-old and had just started back to school. I don't think Gail had much of a childhood. Being familiar with Gail's story, pushed by her mother into movies, ending up an alcoholic, sometimes I feel guilty I couldn't have done something to help her. There was a strain of Cherokee native running in our family; highlighted in Gail's dusky complexion and black hair. She however, possessed a pair of eyes like no other. After all these years I've never forgotten those blue eyes of hers. My aunt Gail; a shooting star burned out in the Hollywood atmosphere!

Charlie Timmons, 2015

Chapter 1
There's nothing to be afraid of

On August 26, 1961, a Saturday night, two women contacted the west Los Angeles police department. They were both worried. Their neighbor, Mrs. Moseley, who lived alone at 1536 Bentley Avenue off Santa Monica Boulevard, hadn't been seen since Thursday evening, when they talked to her through the living room window.[1]

Detective Monahan arrived, questioned the resident that called in, and discovered this wasn't unusual. Ever since Mrs. Moseley moved in eight months ago, she stayed locked up in her home with virtually no visitors.[2] It was a small one room $130 dollar-a-month apartment. If she conversed with her neighbors, it was through a window or a door. The two neighbors, Mrs. Kathrine Foppiano and Mrs. Virginia Darrell were always checking to see if she needed anything.

Occasionally a man could be seen paying a visit to her home.[3] The rumors in the neighborhood was that he was with Alcoholics Anonymous; for Mrs. Moseley was known to have a drinking problem. Mrs. Darrell, who lived two doors down from Mrs. Moseley at 1432 Bentley, and Mrs. Foppiano who resided across from her at 1105 Ohio Street kept a close watch; they weren't nosey or busybodies, it was done out of concern. It seemed the only friends that Mrs. Moseley had were people who looked out for her. Detective Monahan learned from the two women that the lights had been on in Mrs. Moseley's apartment but they had heard no sound or activity.[4]

While waiting outside, Mrs. Foppiano and Mrs. Darrell gathered with a few other neighbors and hoped for the best.[5] But when the ambulance pulled up and a stretcher was taken in, a sense of foreboding enveloped the group. When the stretcher was removed, the worst result had come true.

When detective Monahan returned back outside, he talked some more with Mrs. Darrell. Yes, Mrs. Moseley was a recovering alcoholic. Painting was a hobby she returned to. That's what she did before she was discovered for movies.[6] For Mrs. Moseley was better known as the actress Gail Russell. The Hollywood starlet who starred in movies with John Wayne and Alan Ladd and was the former wife of Guy Madison, the cowboy star of television.

Reporters arrived to gather information, Mrs. Darrell telling them, "I know she had a sincere desire to stop drinking but couldn't. It's a tragic thing. She was a lovely, shy girl with her dark hair, large eyes, and husky voice. Only three months ago she went on a binge and had to be hospitalized for three weeks."[7]

The next day, news of Gail Russell's passing would be in newspapers and broadcasted on radio and television. The tragic end of another actress in Hollywood.

Four-years earlier, Gail attempted to explain her rise and fall saying, "Everything happened so fast. I was a sad character. I was sad because of myself. I didn't have any self-confidence. I didn't believe I had any talent. I didn't know how to have fun. I didn't think I was pretty. I was afraid. I don't know exactly of what—of life I guess."[8]

In the film "Moonrise" Gail's co-star Dane Clark reassures her in one scene: "There's nothing to be afraid of." For Gail Russell there no longer was.

Chapter 2
A Near Gale in the Windy City

Gail Russell was born Elizabeth L. Russell on September 21 or 23, 1921 or 1924 in Chicago, Illinois (depending on what source of information you read). Her parents were George and Gladys Russell.

Right away I wondered about the origin of the name Gail and what the "L" in her middle name stood for. There are several short forms for Elizabeth. Examples like Beth, Eliza, Ellen, and so on. But Gail is not one of them. Betty is however. Perhaps the "L" in her name stood for an abbreviation of Gail. What is even more confusing is that Gail herself once told a movie magazine, "I was born in Chicago on September 23, 1921. I tell my real age now."[1]

Then I remembered, that in doing my research, she had been booked in one of her arrests as Betty Gail Russell, entertainer.[2] And in the 1930 United States Census, Betty L. Russell, age 5, is listed in Cook County, Chicago.[3] Still, there was the unsolved mystery of her middle name. There was only one way to find out for sure. Get a copy of her birth record.

I contacted Cook County with a request for Elizabeth L. Russell born September 21 or 23 in the year 1921 or 1924. Within days a copy arrived and it contained quite a surprise. A child by the name of Betty Gale Russell was born on September 21, 1924 to George and Gladys Russell.[4] There was no Elizabeth or a middle name starting with an "L". All of the biographies and websites like IMDB had it incorrect all those years. It is curious how something like this happened. Often a mistake gets printed once and repeated over and over again. Pretty soon it is accepted as fact. The birth certificate lists father George as 34-years of age. Occupation: assistant manager of a company. His wife Gladys, housewife, age 28. Another child listed as 5-years-old George Jr., named after his father.

Somewhere along the line, Gale was misspelled and Gail took over. Why Gail herself would make such a misstatement about her birthday is curious. Did she actually say it? Quotes in movie magazines are not always accurate. They are created for consumption to give fans a glamorous fantasy world of Hollywood by publicity departments at the studios. At any rate, Gail was born in Chicago spending her early life there.

Her ancestors originally came from Ireland. The name Russell is derived from English, Scottish, and Irish "Rousel," a common Anglo-Norman French nickname for someone with red hair. Her grandfather, Samuel Russell, was born in Canada. His wife was formerly known as Clara Perrin. Like other people searching for a better life, Samuel and Clara had settled in Chicago and started a family. A good sized one. Two daughters: Ada and Josephine. Four sons: Howard, Bertie, Samuel Jr., and George Harrison Russell. Gail's father George was the second oldest son born in 1888. George and his siblings grew up in Utica Township, La Salle County, Illinois.[5]

Her mother, Gladys Barnett, was born in Chicago in 1894. She was the daughter of Lewis Barnett and Susan Barry. Gladys came from a large family like George Russell did. Her siblings included: Lecretia (b.1890), Clarence (b. 1888), Otto (b.1886), Bert (b.1884), Maude (b.1896), Louise (b.1899), and Ruth Emma, (b.1892), grandmother of Charlie Timmons. Gladys spent her formative years in Chicago's Ward 7 of Cook County, Illinois.[6]

The Chicago fire of 1871 had killed nearly 300 people and destroyed roughly three miles of Chicago, leaving over 100,000 people homeless. Despite this horrible calamity, during the turn of the century, Chicago was transitioning into a real metropolis. Almost doubling its population; all types of people came seeking employment. The city offered meat packing, railroading, printing, and garment work to those looking for a job. It was also a thriving manufacturing center.

When Gladys Barnett was a teenager, she found a job selling California fruit in a market near the old Essanay Studios where Charlie Chaplin made his comedies. Early movie stars Tom Mix and Gloria Swanson worked at the studio as well. It was the premier place to make silent movies before they left Chicago for the warmer climates of California.

Gladys had grown into quite an attractive young woman, and it wasn't long before she was offered a screen test. But in fear of losing her job, she declined the offer.[7] It was a decision she would regret for the rest of her life. Later, a second chance to realize this missed opportunity would be given to her, even though it meant living it through her daughter.

By 1918, George Russell had grown up, left home, and began living in a boarding house in Chicago's ward 3. He shared the premises with a dozen other lodgers. Gladys Barnet lived in a similar situation in Chicago's ward 6 with double the number of lodgers. (In 1937, the city was divided into municipal districts called wards.)

George always had a love of music and could play any instrument. He would fill in at band dates when available. He was playing a clarinet in a local orchestra when he met the striking young woman named Gladys. With black hair and sparkling eyes, he was smitten and they soon became a couple. They married, setting up a home in ward 6. George became an auto insurance salesman; Gladys was a housewife and soon to be mother. Their son George Russell Jr. was born on February 7, 1919.

The roaring twenties were just around the corner. The future looked bright for the Russell family and everybody else. In Chicago, the twenties would be a time of wonder and great times. Plenty of fast cars, ready to wear clothes, and the popularity of the radio. But the city also saw the rise of gangland violence and corrupt politicians. Police were in full force; prohibition was the law of the land and bootleggers were everywhere. It was into this atmosphere that the Russells were expecting their second child, she would be named Betty Gale Russell.

The first thing people noticed about the new addition to the Russell family were the eyes. The baby girl had eyes of bright blue. Some people would describe them as a variety of gems, like a blue gemstone. When Gail was growing up people would comment on them. But for Gail, it brought unwanted attention to her. For at the earliest age, she disliked being noticed. Painfully shy, inhibited, and moody, this neurotic child was tormented throughout her life with an agonizing kind of self-consciousness.[8] Gail also suffered from social anxiety. "Until I was twelve, I was so shy you couldn't get me to open my mouth. When my parents had guests, I would run get under the piano and hide there. Whenever I had to recite lessons or speak pieces in school, I behaved like an imbecile. Or I didn't show up."[9] Only after Gail studied the visitors to her home would she come out.

The Russells lived comfortably before the Great Depression hit in a big spacious apartment located on the south side in Hyde Park, Chicago. The apartment was furnished in early American with a grand piano and a big Buick in the garage.

At the age of five, Gail was thin and spindly legged, like a new born Colt. One thing she discovered at such an early age was a love of art. She began sketching on any old piece of paper she could find. Getting her first box of crayons was a joy, with such a variety of colors to choose from. By seven, she began drawing cartoons. In kindergarten, Gail swiped all the little colored pencils, crayons, and paper from school. Later, she was made to return them when found out.

When she turned seven, she requested oil paints instead of water colors. From then on it was her number one choice of art material.

In addition to showing early signs of artistic abilities, Gail also had a bit of the tomboy in her. One time a neighborhood boy invited her over to try his homemade Tarzan swing. Gail gave it a try and ended up breaking her arm, but managed to keep it a secret till the circus left town.

Growing up there was quite a bit of difference between Gail and her older brother George. He was more outgoing and musically inclined like his father. George Jr. was considered special and his parents had high hopes for him. Gail realized at an early age that George was the favored child. Lewis Allen, who later directed Gail in the film "The Uninvited" stated, "She was a sad character, her parents treated her abominably. They had a son and they doted on this boy. And Gail was sort of an afterthought."[10]

Allen must have witnessed an incident or heard rumors for him to make such a statement. Favoritism has a lasting impact on a child's emotional development. The less favored children feel diminished and unfairly treated compared to the favored child, who feels highly valued and especially deserving. The child who is not favored becomes sullen and distant. Not wanting to witness the preferential treatment of her brother, Gail would escape to her bedroom, where she would paint or read and, when permitted, eat her meals. Gladys described her daughter after her discovery in movies as, "a lonely, shy little girl who locked herself away in her room for days at a time, refusing to talk even to her family."[11]

Gail came out of her room though, for she kept a bike that she rode around in Hyde Park with her family. Sometimes she would bring her pet cat perched in a box on the handlebars.

During the summer there was swimming every morning in the lake and occasionally the entire family would go out for walks. When on a walk, Gail always walked ahead of her family, and at times she would be completely silent. Other times, during a walk, she would be the complete opposite.

A family photo taken around this time period shows the Russell family outside their home. People who have seen the picture noticed that Gail is off to the side, while her parents and brother are front and center with the father's arm protectively around the son. Nothing wrong with this, but looking at Gail, who was five-years younger, you wonder what emotions she was experiencing. It could also be that, with her reserved nature, she didn't want to be in the picture in the first place.

In an interview years later, Gail said that she and her brother were not really companionable due to their age difference. She also said that George was close to their mother, but her dad was her best friend.

For her part, Gail counters that she was content as a child saying, "It was a happy childhood actually, and a musical one. My father played about everything: piano, violin, banjo, and guitar. We lived in a small apartment. I played bass drum, my brother the guitar, and dad the violin. I was 9 or 10 then. I remember mother bawling dad out because we'd play so late, she was afraid I wouldn't get enough sleep. Dad used to tell me I could be anything I wanted to be, but I thought he was saying that because he loved me."[12] What's noticeable in this comment is any mention of her mother. In a lot of ways Gail was a lot like her father George, an emotional man at heart.

Gail described herself in those early years saying, "I can't remember a time when I wasn't painfully shy. I don't mean the garden variety shyness most people have, mine was a thousand time worse. I was possessed with an agonizing kind of self-consciousness where I felt my insides tighten into knots. Where my face and hands grew clammy, where I couldn't open my mouth, where I felt impelled to turn and run if I had to meet new people. Isn't it awful? Mother's friends would say, noting about the way I stayed by myself and acted like one struck dumb at meeting strangers. 'She'll be miserable all her life unless she gets over it,' she would say."

"I remember when I was 12 and was invited to my first party. Mother, knowing I would try to back out of going, had me dressed up early in the afternoon believing that my new organdy dress would give me the courage to go. But as the hour for the party drew near, I sat at home trembling, wishing I could disappear. I became so panicky that I began to cast about for an excuse not to go. (Gail found one, helping a blind man sell pencils on the street.) I had a honey of an inferiority complex. School had been a trial to me because of the torture of associating with other children. That's why I took up art, to escape from the necessary adjustments to reality."[13] (Such was Gail's shyness that she preferred to play with one child at a time instead of groups of children.)

To get a break from the Windy City, Gail spent her summers at her Uncle Howard's farm in Ingham County, Michigan. While there she learned to appreciate the fresh climate and an easier way of life. Plus, Howard had two children of his own for Gail to play with and she loved all the different animals and livestock. Gail always had a certain affinity for any type of animal, especially dogs and horses. It seemed that the farm life agreed with Gail. After a summer in the country and a lot of good food she had filled out. The 10-year-old was no longer thin, but chubby and had to wear a size 14 skirt.

Back home in Chicago, Gail quickly trimmed herself back down by roller skating all over the city. She loved to skate to the Piccadilly theatre to watch the latest movies. Years later, she would recall that she went to the movies, "Every single after noon and sat there, watching a movie two or three times. My father would have to come and find me. Once, after a Ginger Rogers movie, my father found me in the street, dancing and singing. It may seem odd that anyone so shy would make a spectacle of herself. But when I felt, I was not me, you see I wasn't really afraid."[14]

After seeing Ginger Rogers in several movies, she became Gail's favorite actress. Gail began keeping a scrap book of Ginger and never in her wildest dreams did she think that someday the two would be in a movie together. Gail enjoyed going to the movies for the same reason other people did; to escape from life into another world. But soon, the world she knew was in for a big change. The Russell family was thinking of making an important decision; to move from Chicago, the place Gail had called home for 12 years and relocate to either California or Florida.

Chapter 3
Fateful Pickup

Like thousands of others, the Russell family struggled during the Great Depression. In the city of Chicago, the situation was extremely severe. The city depended on its manufacturing, which was hit hardest nationwide, and unemployment reached record highs. George always tried to provide well for his family, but it was a hard effort to make ends meet. As an auto bond salesman, he often moved his family from place to place. So, it came as no surprise that George contemplated another move in 1936. This time however, it meant a larger one. Gladys, George Jr., and Gail, who was 12 at the time, helped make the decision.[1] California or Florida? After some serious thought the family decided on California because they had relatives there. Among them, Uncle Bert, and Gladys's sister Emma.

California had been hit hard by the economic collapse, but offered prospects for a better life than Chicago did. Thousands of people made the same choice as the Russells did and headed to California. With its pleasant climate and promise of more jobs, many people were hoping for a better life than before; sadly, not many would find it.

Upon arriving in California, the Russells moved into a little four bedroom house in Glendale. The city of Glendale was the home of the Grand Central Airport, where so many of the people had worked before the Depression hit. The climate was warm, the summers were dry, but never overly hot and the winters were wet but mild. Gail quickly found that she loved California, with its sunshine and smells of lemon and orange blossoms.

Gail attended Wilson Junior High School. As usual, starting a new school is always difficult, but for Gail it was emotionally distressing. Old fears of her social anxiety problems came flooding back. John Wayne, who starred in two movies with Gail sympathized with her saying in an interview years later, "She had an anxiety problem, which I understood because I'd had that when I was a kid."[2] Wayne had another thing in common with Gail, his mother favored his brother. Wayne handled his anxiety as he grew up, Gail never would.

The Russells must not have been happy in Glendale, for the family decided to move back to Chicago for a short time. But in no time, they decided to turn around and head back to California, settling in Santa Monica.³

Santa Monica is a beachfront city on the west coast of Los Angeles, Mar Vista, and Venice. Even with lots of parks, an agreeable climate and aircraft companies that offered jobs, George didn't keep his family there very long. Next, the Russells moved to Van Nuys, where George was employed by Lockheed Aircraft and Gail went to Van Nuys High School. "On my first day at school, being the shy type, I was quite bewildered by all the new faces, all the activity. At the first roll call, the name Russell was announced and a firm young voice answered 'here!' Timidly, I echoed 'here.' The Russell who owned the other young voice turned out to be Jane Russell. She was so different than me, extroverted, confident, and friendly. She took me in tow, taught me the ropes and helped me so much; in ways she never knew. I wouldn't have missed her friendship for the world."⁴

"Jane tried to get me out of my shell. She discovered that the more I thought about going anywhere, the more I had time to work myself into a state of agony over it. So, she would call at the last minute and say, 'Gail, honey my brothers are on their way to pick you up and you're coming with us to a dance. She'd hang up before I could make an excuse. There was only time to dress and before I knew it, I was going on my way."⁵

Gail later transferred to University High School when the Russells moved back to Santa Monica.⁶ At school she continued her lifelong love of art, and dreamed of becoming a commercial artist. Commercial artists create pictures to help promote products for companies such as billboards, print advertisement, product packaging, logos and much more. Commercial art creates a way to show people the product or service by using an image that may catch one's eye. This appealed to Gail with her skill in free-hand drawing and painting.

Although Gail would be referred to as a loner by herself and others who knew her, she could be talked into going to the beach by her classmates. Sometimes on Sunday morning she went with the gang to Santa Monica beach to swim and eat hot dogs. Strolling on the beach barefoot was a joy, and Gail enjoyed the fun of being a teenager, even when she was caught unaware and pushed into the water. Years later, her classmates would recall these memories and comment that Gail's eyes always had a frightened look. "She was the most timorous looking girl in class and her eyes were large and registered fright easily."[7] This look of hers would come in handy when making movies.

Two of those classmates would put into action a life-changing event that would turn Gail Russell's world upside down. Charles Chase and Charles Bates were hitchhiking when a car stopped and picked them up. Chatting on the way, the boys discovered that the driver was a Paramount studio executive by the name of William Meiklejohn. Hearing what he did for a living, they informed him about a beautiful girl in school who should be in movies. She was known as "The Hedy Lamarr of Santa Monica."[8] (Gail always disliked the moniker because she believed herself funny looking.) They said all the boys in Santa Monica were crazy about her, but she wasn't having any part of them.

Meiklejohn sent a memo to Milton Lewis, the head of new talent at Paramount, then got in touch with the school, which turned out to be the wrong one. As it turned out, there were four Russell families with daughters that were students at the school. William had all four girls come to his office; he didn't consider any of them potential movie actresses.

Meiklejohn thought that he had been played for a fool. So, the next time he got some Santa Monica kids in his car he said as much. "Oh, no" they said, "you mean Gail Russell." The kids then told Meiklejohn that Gail went to Santa Monica Tech, not Santa Monica High. A few days later Meiklejohn met with Gail. Realizing that the kids were right about her potential as an actress, Meiklejohn signed her to a $70 dollar a week contract.[9] (The amount is incorrect. It was actually $50.)

Milton Lewis remembered there was some difficulty locating Gail. A phone message was placed on Gail's desk at Sana Monica Tech: "Please call Milton Lewis as Paramount Studios regarding a screen test, H02411, ext. 642. Please call as soon as possible." Gail presumed it was a gag. "I didn't know anything about this. Things like that are always happening in high school. I was minding my own business, getting ready to graduate and find a job as an artist. I threw the note in the waste basket. Then I got to wondering. After school I dug into the basket and got the note and I phoned

Paramount. They did want to see me. I didn't know whether to go or not, but I went."[10]

When Gail arrived home with the note, both of her parents were ecstatic. Her father always knew it would happen to her. Gail expressed her doubts; she alone knew more than anybody else that she wasn't cut out to be a movie actress. That didn't stop her mother. "She practically dragged me there. I had just applied for a job with Bullocks Wilshire department store."[11] Gladys knew better than anyone her daughter's instability. Persuading Gail into a profession she was ill-suited for was not looking out for Gail's interest. Gail and Gladys were aware how she battled with anxiety and was emotionally unstable. But Gladys had blown her chance years before; she wasn't going to this time. Now she was prepared to live her girlhood ambitions through her daughter. Gail, being the dutiful daughter went along, even though it meant not living her own life.

Another factor was the family's financial situation. George Jr. was now away in the Army and work was hard to find for the rest of the family. In fact, things had gotten so bad that the car and most of the furniture had been repossessed and Gail was sleeping on a newspaper covered floor. Looking to cut expenses, the family was preparing to move from their house into a cheaper, three-bedroom apartment. With thoughts of a chance at the big money movie stars make, the decision to get her daughter into movies seemed reasonable to Gladys.

Gladys rushed around making sure Gail had the right dress, then hurried to the studio with Gail in tow. Having no car, Gladys and Gail caught a ride with a neighbor. Walking in the gates of Paramount seemed like a dream come true for Gladys, but it was a nightmare for Gail. At that moment, she probably wished those two classmates had decided not to go to the beach that day or that Mr. Meiklejohn had suffered a flat tire.

Through the arched entrance, with the words Paramount Pictures written across it, Gladys and Gail went. Once inside, they passed offices and huge sound stages that were like military barracks. It must have been an impressive site and no doubt daunting to an 18-year-old high school girl.

Finding herself in Mr. Meiklejohn's office, Gail tensed up like the little girl who used to hide under her parent's piano to avoid meeting new people. Gail recalled him as a kindly man who kept trying to get her to talk. "I just sat there with my teeth in my mouth, but nothing would come out."[12] Gail commented years later about the meeting saying, "I learned later that the talent head liked me because I seemed different than most of the rah-rah personality girls he'd seen. He was actually intrigued with my shy manners—thought it natural and girlish."

Milton Lewis expressed no doubts about Gail. "I never doubted the studio wouldn't be ok with a contract. Gail had that very special star like quality mixed with artistic sensitivity. I knew it the minute she walked into my office. She was radiant to look at with a touch of mystery about her."[13] Milton wasted no time setting up a screen test.

Going back home, Gail felt uneasy and relieved to get out of the place. She wished she was back in art class at Santa Monica Tech. But three days later she found herself back at Paramount for her big screen test. Gail thought back to the time in grade school during Thanksgiving when she was in a play and couldn't speak her lines; this time she did better. Milton Lewis said, "Gail responded well to direction in her test, (a scene from the movie Love Finds Andy Hardy) from my assistant, William Russell."[14] After the test, Gail was offered a seven-year contract which provided for annual raises or revisions and a starting salary of $50 a week.

Gail's mother told her, "Take it, we need the money."[15] The deal may have looked promising at the time, but Gladys had no idea how a big studio like Paramount operated. All of the major heads of the studio had one goal; to make and save money. Adolph Zukor, the head of Paramount was no exception. One strategy Zukor used to save money was to sign attractive young people at the lowest possible salaries. He would then co-star the most promising ones with established names. If the newcomer failed to ignite after six months or a year, he or she was dropped from their contract with a minimal financial loss.[16] Gail was a good example of the way Paramount worked. Taking everything into account about how Gail's life ended up, one wishes Paramount had dropped her. In the years ahead, the life of Gail Russell would undergo many changes, both professional and personally; from an innocent teenage girl full of trust to a weary, misused woman. "Paramount didn't know how to handle her," reflected John Wayne. "They broke her spirit."[17]

Chapter 4
By Starlight

It may be hard to believe that a prestigious studio like Paramount began in a horse barn, but it did. Founder Adolf Zukor was a Hungarian immigrant in 1903 when his cousin asked him for a loan. Several investors were needed to expand a chain of arcade theatres. These theatres specialized in the early moving pictures of Thomas Edison. Zukor loaned the money to his cousin with the stipulation that he open one himself. By 1912 Zukor had established the famous French Players or Celebrated Players studio that produce both short and feature length productions. Its first release was the French film, *Les Amours de la reine Elisabeth*, starring the famous actress, Sarah Bernhardt, and Lou Tellegen.

The studio was located in New York where conditions weren't always favorable for making films. In 1915 Zukor relocated the company to Melrose Avenue in Hollywood. The primary goal of the studio was to bring well-known stage actors to the movie screen. By 1916, Zukor's company had grown, and he was a very successful producer and director. It was around this time that he decided to merge the French Players studio with Jesse L. Lasky's Feature Play Company, which eventually became Paramount Pictures.

Several people at Paramount played important roles in Gail's early career. Executive producer Buddy DeSylva, director Lewis Allen, screenwriter Charlie Brackett, and drama coach William Russell all had a hand in Gail's early development and wasted no time in getting her started.

To start with, she had voice lessons for four hours a day. She also had to learn how to walk gracefully, which was a chore because she was slightly pigeon toed. To correct the problem, she had to walk up and down a long stage and a staircase with her feet pointed out and a book balanced on her head. At first, her walk was hurried; her shoulders were hunched, and she held her head down in what seemed like an effort to pass by unnoticed. But after a few lessons and some coaching, she gained confidence and improved immensely.

During this time, Gail also took dancing lessons, fencing lessons, and riding lessons. Of all the required training, riding was her favorite. Riding brought her in contact with horses and rekindled her lifelong love of animals. With all the preparations, her days were like a whirlwind, and Gail did her best to compress all the training into the shortest time possible.[1]

In addition to training, Gail had to pose for dozens of still pictures for publicity buildup. Years later, Gail could still recall the embarrassment of walking in a bathing suit holding an umbrella, while actors broke for lunch, among them Alan Ladd and Bing Crosby passing by. Gail experienced further discomfort from the make-up department. This was a girl who had never worn make-up of any kind. And she particularly disliked having her eye brows plucked. She did however, like having her hair done and was amazed at what the stylist could do with a person's hair; shape it, mold it, and straighten up any type of hair.

Not every new starlet is noticed on a movie lot. So many come and go. In Gail's case, she couldn't help but attract attention. With raven black hair and an unusual shade of blue eyes, people couldn't help but notice. For a girl who disliked being the center of attention, this was unsettling. People who talked to her found her strangely melancholy. Almost as if she didn't really want to be there. Of course, they didn't know how right they were. Gail didn't want to be there and would have given anything just to be at a drawing board.

Paramount intended to get her started right away. Gail discovered that it was a rush and she was always in a hurry working at the studio. There was no time to waste. Getting the product filmed, packaged, and delivered to the waiting public was all that counted.

A few months later, Gail was scheduled to appear in her first movie called, "Henry Aldrich Gets Glamour." The movie was released on April 30, 1943 and was part of a series of comedy films that starred Jimmy Lydon as Henry, a blundering teenager who was always getting into jams. Lydon was only a year older than Gail but had been acting since 1937. He began in the Broadway play "Western Waters" and honed his craft for the next couple of years. In 1939 he moved to Hollywood seeking movie roles. Jimmy played the title character in the movie "Tom Brown's School Days" with Cedric Harwicke. During the years 1941 and 1944, he was under contract to Paramount playing the screechy voiced Henry Aldrich. Each movie began with the trademark cry from Henry's mother, "Henry, Henry Aldrich!" to which Henry would reply, "Coming mother." Imitated in school yards all over, the Aldrich films competed with the Andy Hardy films of Mickey Rooney.

Paramount considered these films to be a good training ground for many young Paramount contract players. It was only natural that Gail got her feet wet in a vehicle of this type.

How well Gail slept the night before reporting to work for her movie debut is not hard to guess. Anytime she had to undergo a public display of any kind, she was sent into a panic. Now reporting to the sound stage, she was doing her best to control herself and her fear. First, there was a rehearsal of a scene before shooting. William Russell, the drama coach worked with her patiently. Years later, William gave his recollection of first meeting Gail saying, "The first time I saw Gail she was a frightened little rabbit. She came with her mother and didn't say a word. In reply to a question, she just nodded or shrugged her shoulders. I was intrigued because I never met a girl who didn't talk. Gail's fears," said William, "is a fear of the unknown. Her first brush with acting was like being in the dentist chair, I had to drill it out of her. But when she passed her first test, her confidence started to grow. When she received a small contract, it grew more. It was six months before she had her first part, and we had lessons every day. She didn't want to do 'Henry Aldrich Gets Glamour.' She didn't feel ready. She's a perfectionist, and she'd feel foolish. She's so afraid that people will laugh at her that she remains silent and would rather have them think she is dumb."[2]

(Gail's fears of acting were so great that William would have to meet Gail at the front gate of the studio to escort her in. William waited off camera to encourage her before shooting. He held her hand and tried to inspire her to believe in herself, while she did her best to overcome her fears and tears.)

Gail approached film work with the same intensity as her art work, but there was one major difference. An art studio had a relaxed slow-paced feel to it. A movie lot soundstage was the complete opposite. Jimmy Lydon recalled her first day on the set. "She came in and got into make-up and her costume and came on set. She was so scared that she was trembling. The first thing she had to do was a kind of medium shot of her on the telephone talking to me. I was going to be off stage from her, doing the other side of the conversation. Well, we began to rehearse and she started to get nervous, started to tighten up. We finally said, 'what the hell, we'll try a shot.' The cameras turned and the guy hit the sticks and got out of there, and Hugh Bennett said, 'action!' She got half the first lines out and she started to cry. She was so nervous, absolutely scared to death."[3] Luckily, Gail's first director responded with kindness and understanding and recognized her initial frightful introduction to filmmaking.

Hugh Bennett was a former film editor who directed all of the Henry Aldrich pictures. Lydon said he was just the nicest man in the world. He was the kind of director Gail needed for her first picture. She would reveal in an interview that filming the picture was a terrifying experience. "I can hardly remember it," she said. "When I went over the role with William Russell, it seemed possible, well almost possible. But, on the set with the director shouting and the lights blazing and the cameras threatening, I'd go deaf, really. They'd tell me what to do and I simply didn't hear. I'd try desperately to listen and all I did was wish I was dead."[4]

Gail's character, Virginia Lowery, is the most beautiful girl in school and keeps turning Henry down. But when Henry wins a Hollywood contest and goes out with a movie star, Virginia, and the rest of the girls in school take interest in Henry. The movie wasn't only the debut of Gail Russell; it also featured the actress Diana Lynn, who had already made three movies. Diana played the girl who had a crush on Henry, but he ignored her most of the time. Diana was a former pianist and became one of the few close friends Gail made in Hollywood.

Gail's first picture was completed and would always be memorable to her. "The first time I ever danced with a boy in my life was with William Blees in a scene we did for 'Henry Aldrich Gets Glamour,' my first picture. This was the first time I ever wore high heels too. I'd never been to a dance before. When someone would ask me, I'd lock myself in my room with a book and eat graham crackers. It was that way through my teens. During the years when most girls are interested in parties, proms, sororities, and boys, I stayed by myself through a positive fear of meeting people. I tried, several times, to force myself to attend school affairs but at the last minute my legs would turn to water. Once I got as far as the door of a party, but when I heard the music and laughter inside, panic seized me. I turned and ran home, locking myself in my room. Another time a friend took me by the hand and forced me to attend a party. I sat in the corner all evening absolutely petrified, wishing in my heart that I could get up and mingle with the others. But the simple act of

saying 'hello' to any of the guests was a torture. I felt that everyone was staring at me; that my slip was showing or there was a run in my stockings. I would look with envy at the group of girls who gathered after school, walking home together, or stopping in at the ice cream parlor, a gay laughing bunch. I could no more bring myself to join them than I could fly. So, I used to walk home alone."[5]
"I didn't care for clothes. I had them but I didn't want them. Naturally I didn't, since I didn't go anywhere, except the movies. Otherwise, I always came straight home after school, went to my room and read or drew. The first day on set I sat on the sidelines, trembling. I was so scared."[6]

Watching the movie today, she looks no better or worse than the other performers.

When Gail arrived home after her first day, her parents could see that she was in an emotionally agitated state. It's easy to imagine that she pleaded with them not to go back. The reply from her parents was usually that it would get better or to remind her that the first day is always the worst. (Years later, Gail said she stuck with acting mainly because of her father, because he was so thrilled. The minute she would get home from work, he'd back her into a corner and ask about the day's happenings.)

A week later, Gail received her first paycheck from the studio. After all the deductions, her $50 salary had turned into .50 cents. She would have made more as a painter. Gail framed the check and hung it on her wall, keeping it for the rest of her life.

Though Gail's part in her first movie had been small, she received good notices. "When Gail Russell faced Hollywood cameras for the first time, she was insulted, pushed from the fence, her dress torn, stockings smeared with grease and her beautiful brunette hair disheveled."[7]

The next movie for Gail was the former Broadway play, "The Lady in the Dark." Paramount had spent a lot of money buying the rights to the play and was hoping for a big return on their money. Adapted for the screen, most of the music by Kurt Weill and Ira Gershwin was cut out. Ginger Rogers, who had brokered a three picture deal with Paramount was cast to play the starring role of Liza Elliott. Mitchell Leisen was hired as the director and Buddy DeSylva was hired as the executive producer.

Shooting began in December 1942. Behind the scenes the director, Mitchell Leisen and Ginger Rogers clashed often over the movie. It was a complex plot, with flashbacks and psychoanalysis of the main character, Liza Elliott the editor of *Allure magazine*, played by Rogers.

Having a woman in charge of the office creates conflict for the men in the office. After Liza undergoes psychoanalysis, she discovers the reason she is unhappy, anxious, and depressed is because she has been rejected by her narcissistic and indifferent mother. In one flashback from her childhood, Liza talks of, "that bad feeling, running to her room to get away from everyone, never going to dances or parties, building a wall around yourself, never to get hurt again." Does this sound familiar? Reads like a page from Gail Russell's early life.

Gail could hardly believe she was going to work with her favorite actress. It didn't seem that long ago when she was roller skating to the theater in Chicago to view Ginger's latest movie.

When she finally met Ginger she admitted, "I was frantic. I thought I am going to faint; I will run away and hide. Then Ginger Rogers came over to me, put her arm around me, took me into her dressing room, gave me tea, and went over the script with me. We talked about art, music, and books. Best of all, she told me how scared she had been when she first got into pictures. That visit with Ginger was, so to speak, a turning point in relaxing me."[8]

Gail regaled Ginger with a story of a time she and her mother attended the Santa Anita races and saw Ginger in a box. She could even describe the dress that Ginger wore that day, much to Ginger's amusement. Artists have a memory for such detail. She even drew cartoons of Ginger that the actress put on her mirror.

Gail's part in the film was a girl named Barbara. In a flashback scene, she steals a boyfriend from Ginger's character Liza. The scene required Barbara to dance the Charleston. Ginger was only too happy to teach her. Gail had a fractured toe but wasn't about to turn down a dancing lesson from one of the best female dancers of the day. "If Ginger likes me, maybe I'm not too bad," mused Gail. "Now whenever Gail finds a newcomer in her pictures, she goes out of her way to help her. She feels she is repaying her debt to Ginger," said acting coach William Russell.

Notwithstanding all the help that Ginger gave Gail, she still had to battle her severe stage fright. The director, Mitchell Leisen, described his recollections of working with Gail. "Ginger insisted we use Gail Russell as Barbara, the girl who steals Liza's boyfriend right after she sang 'My Ship.' The poor girl was gorgeous but she had hysterics every time the camera started to turn. She only had a couple lines, but it took us almost two days to get those shots. Ginger felt so sorry for her that she tried to work with her and help her as much as she could. She was a neurotic character and I'm not surprised she became an alcoholic."[9]

Nature had blessed Gail with rare beauty but cursed her with unstable behavior.

"Lady in the Dark" was a hit when released in 1944. Critics and fans had differing opinions on the movie but it did well at the box office. When it opened at Paramount Theater in Times Square, twenty three thousand people paid $1 each to see it. It was the biggest opening day in the history of the theater; grossing almost $123,000 at the end of opening week.

Gail would always have fond memories of her times with Ginger Rogers. She kept in her scrapbook the following note sent by Rogers: "My dear Girl? How's my favorite pupil? You're the right kind of pupil to have as I don't have to do anything about it but address you as such anyway, we can pretend can't we? I just loved the drawing you enclosed in your note. You are a darn clever girl and if you aren't careful, you're going to have so many accomplishments you aren't going to know which one to enjoy. As for that laugh, you are definitely going to get one-my nose is sunburned and I have so many freckles I look like a bowl of cornflakes. You tell those people at Paramount they had better treat you right or I shall conjure up some thunder, they'll never forget. Tell them they should give you a pretty dressing room as they should start spoiling you right away. After you've worked too hard, it becomes difficult to appreciate spoiling. Be good and God bless you. Affectionately, Ginger."[10]

Gail had made appearances in two films so far. Gail's debut started with a supporting part in her first movie, a small walk on role in her next. But number three would be the role that would change her life. For some people this role would have been a sign of good luck, but for Gail it may have been bad luck.

Dorothy Macardle wrote a popular novel titled: "Uneasy Freehold." The plot of the novel concerned a brother and sister who purchased a house named Windward home off the coast of Southern England, not knowing that it is haunted. The ghost of the house is determined to kill a young girl, Stella Meredith. The brother and sister solve the mystery and rescue the girl from death.

Macardle was an Irish writer, novelist, playwright, and historian. Macardle's passion for politics had brought her notoriety. During Ireland's Civil War, she was arrested by the Royal Irish Constabulary because she supported the Republican side. She held strong views for Ireland's independence. It was when she was in prison that she began writing ghost stories. Her novel became a Literary Guild selection when it was published in 1942. Paramount bought the rights, and producer Buddy DeSylva chose Charlie Brackett to write a screenplay. Charlie Brackett was a talented screenwriter and producer who, when teamed with Billy Wilder, was considered one of Hollywood's premier screenwriting teams.

One of the first things that Brackett did was work with playwright Dodie Smith. Dodie was born and raised in Lancaster, England and was an only child. Dodie's grandfather and uncle would read Shakespeare to her between trips to the local theater. As a result of this early exposure to literature, she wrote her first play at the age of ten. In 1939, she married Alec Beesley. When WWII broke out, her husband registered as a conscientious objector. Because of legalities associated with this, Dodie and her husband moved to California. There she found work at Paramount writing screenplays.

Brackett started working with Dodie in September 1942 on the script for the "The Uninvited" which was based on "Uneasy Freehold." As the script was taking shape, Brackett approached Alfred Hitchcock to see if he was interested. "He is a monstrous egoist who, when I mentioned the need of having real people and real emotions in 'The Uninvited,' suddenly said, 'My pictures have always been weak on real people and real love stories,' as if I had been hinting at that fact. I found him funny and likeable."[11]

Ultimately, Hitchcock had other commitments and was unavailable. Director Mitchell Leisen was also brought up. Meanwhile Billy Wilder was having doubts about the whole project. Universal Studios was known for horror movies, not Paramount. A ghost story would be right up their alley but not Paramounts. Wilder was ready to leave the screenwriting up to someone else because he wanted to begin a career in directing. Brackett was also veering away from screenwriting towards producing. But regardless of what paths they intended for their respective careers, they completed "The Uninvited" by January 1943.

DeSylva wanted "The Uninvited" produced by March 1943. The first major direction was to choose a director. Brackett talked to Lewis Allen. Similar to Dodie Smith, Allen was originally from England. When he moved to the United States, Lewis became a stage director in New York. When the war came along, he met DeSylva who offered him a job at Paramount. He learned how to direct Hollywood movies from directors Preston Sturges and Mark Standrich. Allen's recollection of being offered to direct "The Uninvited" were as follows: "Charlie Brackett, who was Billy Wilder's partner, was a wonderful man, one of the nicest human beings I've ever known. Charlie said to me one day, 'Lew, I've bought a book called 'Uneasy Freehold' and we're developing a script. I think you'd be the right director for it.' So, he talked to Buddy DeSylva about me and Buddy said, 'Delighted. You can have Lew direct it.' That's how I got to direct "'The Uninvited.'"[12]

Allen's first feature film would benefit from some of Paramount's top technical people such as academy award winning photographer, Charles Lang and Farciot Edouart, who was an expert in special effects.

Since a director was now chosen, casting could start. DeSylva told Brackett he wanted to make a low budget picture using a new actress. He expected the popularity of the movie to be based on the success of the novel's popularity. The role of Stella was one of the key roles in the script. It required a girl with haunting vulnerability. The right actress could make the film, the wrong one could break it. Helen Walker was the first to be tested. Brackett found her, "Appalling, long necked, awkward, and a wretched actress."[13] June Lockhart was next up. She read the part well and Brackett was impressed. She was attractive in her own way but the front office wanted someone who would really grab the attention of the movie audience. Next, Brackett gave Barbara Britton a look see. Still, this wasn't what he was looking for.

Charlie Brackett recalled it was the director, Lewis Allen, who finally solved the problem of a lead actress that everyone thought would fit the role. "While looking through a Paramount Casting book, Allen stumbled on the picture of a contract actress by the name of Gail Russell. He had her brought to the office. Charlie and Lewis were knocked out by her beauty. Also present was Frank Partos, a screenwriter working with Dodie Smith. Together, they went and saw some Henry Aldrich films with her, and she wasn't bad. Not a brilliant actress, but something which can really dazzle the backers, provided director Allen can squeeze any kind of performance out of her."[14]

Allen wasn't very enthusiastic about using Gail Russell because of her lack of experience. The next day she came in and tried to read a scene with Allen and Brackett. Despite spending the previous day memorizing and rehearsing the material, she blew her lines and mispronounced her words. In an odd way, she inadvertently seemed to possess the very character traits of the role she was auditioning for, frightened, inhibited, and beautiful. Allen recalled it as, "Pretty bad."[15] (Screenwriter Billy Wilder supposedly told Allen, "You're welcome to her. I had a terrible time with her. Gail did a tiny part in a movie before this.")

Finally, after much deliberation, Gail was the final choice for the part of Stella Meredith.

The studio wasted no time. Gail was given evening gowns to try on. This would be the first time in her life that she ever wore one. William Russell, her drama coach who adored her, told Brackett she wasn't afraid of him or Lewis Allen. She was not even afraid of the part of this movie. Gail did say she was afraid of the director Sidney Lanfield. Lanfield, a former jazz musician turned director, was known for directing the comedies Bob Hope had made for Paramount. If Gail Russell was afraid of Lanfield, it wasn't for long. Walter Reed, a character actor who worked with Gail, witnessed an incident between the two saying, "Gail Russell gave it to him, Lanfield used to keep a little riding crop with him and he goosed her [touching her buttocks]. And man, she grabbed that thing and hit him across the face with it!"[16]

Gail was discovering the ways of Hollywood. She would meet many types of men in the studio. Some were well-mannered gentlemen. But there were many others that roamed the studios who were coarse, vulgar predators on the make and looking to take advantage of the young, inexperienced starlets.

Brackett still had to sell the executives of Paramount on Gail Russell as the choice for lead lady. He took test footage to William Meiklejohn. Brackett sat with him watching June Lockhart first, a total flop. Next, he watched Gail. After the test, he said to Meiklejohn, "Isn't that gal grand?" Meiklejohn said she had a common voice, was inexperienced, and most of the people in the projection room agreed with him. The part required an English accent since the setting of the movie was taking place on the coast of England. Even Allen was not hearty in his support. Nevertheless, Brackett said, "I stuck to supporting the girl and it was finally agreed that she should have diction lessons for three days and then make a recording of the speeches."[17]

Three days later, Brackett, his secretary, and Dodie Smith walked to the projection room and showed them the Helen Walker test and the Gail Russell test. They all much preferred Helen Walker, thinking her beautiful. Brackett resigned himself to the idea that he was insane to consider Russell for the part, which brought on a depressed mood.

Putting together a picture is a strain most of the time. Stop and go. Start all over again. The public sees the finished project. Not all the effort behind the scenes. The sweat and the tears. All the pressure to get a movie completed on time and on budget. But when it is finished, a tremendous sense of accomplishment for all the people involved: producers, directors, technical workers, writers, actors, and actresses showcasing the material to the best of their ability.

Miriam Greene, an English diction coach, worked hard with Gail. She put the young actress in a projection room watching classic films like, "Pygmalion," "Rebecca," and "The Young Mrs. Pitt." Exhausted, she fell asleep.

Gail learned in time that the studios weren't always concerned with the health of an actress. Getting a film done was their goal. When Brackett saw Gail in rehearsal, he was surprised at how well she did. A recording of her voice was carried to Buddy DeSylva. He was still pushing for Helen Walker but after listening to the recording, Buddy approved Gail for the part of Stella Meredith. Gail was so excited and nervous. Throughout her film career, Gail Russell could rise to the occasion when others gave up.

Now that Gail secured the part of Stella, the movie was almost ready to begin filming. Most of the parts were finalized early in the process. After Gail was chosen, all that was left to pick out was a dog, a cat, and a squirrel. For these parts, Brackett chose a Cairn terrier who was in the Air Force, a cat that goes anywhere it's told, a squirrel that had been in the business eight-years and Ray Milland.

Acting since 1929, Milland worked in British films and stage productions. This Welsh cavalryman would have a long and varied career, including winning an Oscar in 1945 for his role in "The Lost Weekend." Before that success, Milland had gone through some hard times. In 1934, after an interview for the position of an assistant manager for a gas station, he passed Paramount Studios. Milland met a casting director, Joe Egil, who offered him a part in a film. Other small parts followed until he was loaned out to Universal Pictures for the film "Three Smart Girls." After that, Milland returned to Paramount to co-star with Dorothy Lamour in "The Jungle Princess." The movie was a huge success and Paramount rewrote his contract to update him to leading man status.

Milland was to play the part of Rick Fitzgerald, a music critic and composer. The part of his sister was to be played by Ruth Hussey. This former model worked in summer stock and radio. She was spotted by a talent scout for MGM and soon had roles in movies, most notably "The Philadelphia Story." How she obtained a role in "The Uninvited" was unusual. "I was in New York for some reason or another," said Hussey "and my agent contacted me and wanted to know if I would play the part. It had been a book and I don't know if it was called 'The Uninvited,' I don't think it was. But I think there was another title, which I might think of and might not. 'The Uninvited Guest,' maybe that was it. I don't know. Well, anyway, I got the book and I came back on the train to do the part. In those days, you would be on a train for, I think it was three nights and two days, or two days and three nights, or whatever. So, I had a compartment and started to read the book. I was in bed by this time and really began to feel eerie. I didn't feel as if there were spooks around or anything, but I felt funny. I had been reading all of this stuff, so I thought, '*I'll finish it tomorrow*!' and I left the light on all night. Isn't that crazy? So, I finished the story the next day."[18]

Donald Crisp, a versatile supporting actor, played the important role of Stella Meredith's grandfather. Crisp did it all in his film career going back to the silent days. Crisp became a close friend of the legendary director D.W. Griffin, from who he learned much.
Griffin, interviewed in 1948, was asked to name the top performers in movies. He names "The daintiest, sultry-eyed beauty that Russell girl-not Jane, but Gail."

When Crisp started to be a director himself, he made movies with Buster Keaton and Douglas Fairbanks. In 1915, Crisp sold his eleven acre ranch where now stands Paramount Studios. Crisp won an Oscar for best supporting actor in 1941 for "How Green Was My Valley."

Cornelia Otis Skinner and Alan Napier rounded out the rest of the cast. Skinner wrote humorous short pieces for magazines and character sketches that she acted out in one woman plays on stage. She would figure into Gail Russell's career after the movie. Napier is another actor with a long list of credits beginning in England and transitioning into America. Alfred the butler in the TV series "Batman" is what people remember him for. The parts that both played were small but very important to the plot. Gail's mother in the movie, played by Elizabeth Russell, made an appearance as the ghost.

Now that the cast was all set, the shooting could begin. Director Allen and his camera crew already shot some footage of California's northern coast, above San Francisco near Fort Ross. Fort Ross was a former Russian colony dating back to 1812. Early settlers to the region made a living in the fur trade. It was also the home of the first windmills in California. This location was chosen to double for the Devonshire coast of England, where the story was to take place.

April 15, 1943 was the first day scheduled for filming. Gail was on the set but all of the scenes involved Milland and Hussey. Brackett admired Milland saying, "He behaved beautifully all day, was sweet to Gail (who didn't play today) and cooperative with the director Allen. Charlie Lang, the photographer, was long lighting the set. I had time to fret wildly: our characters were wrong; they couldn't have been left in a house; the house was wrong; the lines were wrong-enough to take any pleasure out of the project. Hussey looked well, read the lines a little too fliply. She and I went to my office and read through the remainder of the scenes she completed and I heard her idea for the end, which may be an improvement though I doubt it."[19] The first day had a rough beginning, but nothing that couldn't be remedied.

Brackett started to correct things, starting with the look of the sets. Brackett viewed the daily rushes after each shooting which always took him on a roller coaster of emotions. Up one moment, down the next. On April 20, he stayed on the set most of the morning, watching breathlessly while Whiskey the cat went through a scene, which he did twice like an angel, aided by a dish of fish and cries of "kitty, kitty, kitty" between dialogue.[20]

Rudd Weatherwax trained animals to be used in pictures, including "The Uninvited." The most famous animal he trained was the dog used in "Lassie."

The next few days Brackett observed the scenes being shot with Gail. "She was in hideous clothes, giving an amateur and adenoidal performance." Gail was frequently in tears. Men on the picture worried that it was the wrong time of the month for her to have worked. William Russell, her acting coach, telephoned her mother, who reported that she had woken up with a sore throat since last week. It turned out that she was sulking because the director, Allen, made Gail wear a hat in a scene that she did not want to wear. The first scene on location for Gail was so windy that they had to sew the back of her hat to her collar.

On May 4, Gail was in a good mood, but when Brackett viewed the rushes from the day before, it showed her, cross, pouty, and thoroughly unattractive. "God help the directors and producers who have to handle her in the future,"[21] Brackett would later say. The director Allen concurred saying, "She could only do about five or six lines and then she'd burst into tears. She was scared to death. Well, Ray Milland and I coaxed her along and we made the picture in bits and pieces. We'd do half a page...then another half...and so on. So, we 'manufactured a performance.' Donald Crisp was the reverse. He thought it was amateur night. Working with this unknown actress, he was just brusque with her, that's all."[22]

What Crisp and Allen didn't comprehend was that Gail didn't want to be there in the first place. Instead, she would much rather be working on a sketch for a potential client in a commercial art company. To get a satisfactory performance out of her was going to take more than a bowl of fish.

Getting "The Uninvited" completed was of the uppermost importance to all involved. Gail wanted to cooperate but due to her emotional state, she was fighting an uphill battle. Ray Milland would rehearse and encourage Gail every day, along with William Russell. Milland deliberately blew takes to give Gail time to settle down. Finally, a "No visitors" set was arranged with screens put up to block the view of all the people watching her. When Ruth Hussey was asked about Gail's shy nature she commented, "I guess she was. As I remember she didn't do much rehearsing. She had a coach, a Paramount coach, and he worked on all the scenes, and then she would come in and we would just shoot it. Well, maybe there was a little rehearsal or something. She must have been nervous, because I heard it so many times, but she was fine on the set and there was no carrying on or histrionics. She just played her scenes and played them beautifully."[23] Hussey was either covering up for Gail or being charitable. Everyone else connected to the picture says the complete opposite.

Eventually Gail settled down and started to make a marked improvement in her acting. If people around the set wondered what caused the change, they soon discovered why. According to Lewis Allen, "Things didn't get much better until the head of makeup and the hairdresser took her to a little bar across the street. And they introduced her to liquor. At the time we did 'The Uninvited' she'd never had a drink in her life. They wanted to give her confidence and after she started going with them and having a drink at night, she had a little more courage during the day. She was looking forward to the drink in the evening, I guess."[24]

I'm sure these people believed that they were helping Gail, a 19-year-old girl with virtually no history in the movie industry, to cope with the demands of movie making. Unfortunately, they set her on a path of destruction that she would never recover from. So many actors and actresses take up drinking to deal with the stress of standing in front of the camera; Gail was no exception. She found a golden elixir to make all her fears vanish. In the end, it would take away a whole lot more.

Now that Gail had found a way to get through the picture, shooting was running more smoothly until June 8. That day brought a near disaster. Brackett was informed that "The double" in the cliff scene was injured. The girl clinging to a tree root had been unable to hang on and had fallen to the net, amid a shower of stones which almost killed her. "I raced to the set to learn the facts: she had fallen but the rocks weren't real rocks and though her neck was cut and her arm injured, she'd wanted to make the shot again."[25] It was later decided to use some of this footage in the movie. By early July, shooting on the movie was almost finished. Brackett listened to Victor Young's music score for the picture and found it superb. His rendition of "Stella by Starlight" is a classic. Gail never got tired of hearing it the rest of her life.

All that was left was dubbing some scenes. Dubbing is the process used in post-production where additional recordings are mixed with the original tracks to create the final cut. Brackett couldn't believe it was the same girl. "Gail began and dubbed pretty successfully until about 4:00 a.m., when her voice gave out. The change in the girl is fantastic-her assurance, her poise, which have replaced the abnormal ingrown shyness."[26] Did he know where this change of behavior came from? Brackett and the director Allen were friends. Brackett wasn't naïve; he knew about the café across the street from Paramount that served drinks. Surely, he inquired about the change in Gail's mood to Allen. In later years, when Allen gave interviews reminiscing about Gail Russell, he would break out laughing. Did Allen and the other people working on "The Uninvited" find it amusing to get an innocent young girl tipsy so she could perform and get the movie finished in time?

When "The Uninvited" was ready for a sneak preview, theater goers were given cards to fill out and write their comments on. They could comment on anything having to do with the movies such as the actors, actresses, the setting, or the plot of the movie. Brackett went to the first preview held in Inglewood, California and commented, "The title flashed on the screen, wild applause for Milland's name, amusement at the squirrel chase, (first scene Allen shot), interest in Gail, a cackle of laughter for the fading flowers, some nervous laughter for Milland's waking and the whole haunting scene. Then, beautiful breathless absorption in the story, gasps, screams as Rick tried to reach Stella before she got to the cliff. As satisfactory a reaction as a preview ever got!"[27]

Next it was shown in Glendale where Gail and her family lived when they first moved to California. To Gail, it seemed a long time ago. Brackett found this audience different than the one in Glendale. "More moronic than last time, filled with children and sailors and kids given to whistling. They spotted Ruth Hussey, who was there before the picture began, and Gail, and began to scramble for autographs. The picture began and I thought we were going to have trouble, then the picture started to grip them and played just as well as before, possibly a shade better. The cards were superb, mentioning Gail over and over, and I drove home with a curious feeling of degradation, as though I'd succeeded in scaring the hell out of a school of backward children."[28] The enthusiastic responses to the movie and a new star like Gail was exactly what the studio was striving for.

If the movie absorbed and gripped the audience, it had good reason too. It begins with Rick Fitzgerald and his sister Pamela hiking along the coastal shore. Spotting an oceanfront villa (Windward House) their pet terrier takes chase after a squirrel into the house. Once inside, they give it the once over and fall in love with its quaintness. The owner is Commander Beach. He is cantankerous and strangely guarded about the house.

Rick decides to buy the house but the Commander's granddaughter, Stella Meredith tries to prevent her grandfather from selling. Beach accepts the first offer from Rick, a low one. Rick and his sister are suspicious until Beach informs them about the history of the house. His daughter Mary was killed on the cliffs overlooking the house years ago. Another couple lived there but found it unsettling and left.

Rick and Pamela move in and set up housekeeping but strange things keep happening. There are cries in the night and pets exhibit bizarre behavior. Glancing out the window one day, Rick sees Stella transfixed on the edge of the cliff before running off. Shortly after, Rick invites her over one evening. The housekeeper reports seeing a ghost and soon after Stella becomes possessed. She makes a mad dash for the cliff but Rick saves her. Stella is then cared for by the village doctor who tells Rick and Pamela the shameful history of Windward House. Stella's father, an artist, had an affair with a gypsy model named Carmel. After the birth of Stella, Carmel returns to Windham House where she kidnaps baby Stella. Carmel then attempts to throw the baby from the cliff but Mary intervenes. She saves Stella, but in the process falls to her death over the edge of the cliff. Terrified, Carmel runs into the stormy night only to be found the next morning dying from pneumonia.

Rick then tries to hold a séance but it fails when Stella becomes possessed. The spirits of both Carmel and Mary are battling for control of Stella.

Stella is sent away to a retreat named after her mother. Rick and Pamela pursue Stella and confront the woman in charge who does her best to mislead them. Meanwhile, the village doctor uncovers a diary that reveals that Carmel is really Stella's mother. Mary only claimed parenthood to salvage her family's reputation. So, when Carmel journeyed back to Windham House, she was trying to reclaim the daughter that was taken from her. When a struggle for baby Stella ensued, Mary went over the cliff.

Once released from the retreat, Stella returns home to find her grandfather dying. Mary's ghost materializes and tries to urge Stella to jump off the cliff. Stella arrives at the cliff but in a hair raising scene, Rick saves her before she goes over the edge. Now that Stella knows the truth about her parentage, the spirit of Carmel disappears but the ghost of Mary is still in Windham House. Rick confronts her, reminding her that the truth is known and she is powerless. Laughing at her sudden loss of force, she disappears forever. Rick and Stella can live happily ever after.

"The Uninvited" was successful and everyone connected with it was pleased. It certainly helped the careers of the people in it. Ruth Hussey said, "It was a good role and an interesting story, it was so nice to work with Ray Milland and little Gail Russell."[29] The uncomfortable feelings created by fame from her small roles the previous year were now amplified as Gail Russell became a bona fide movie star. Years later, Ava Gardner, who rose to fame much the same way as Gail would say, "What I would really like to say about stardom is it gave me everything I never wanted."[30] Gail Russell would find this to be truer than anyone could have ever imagined.

Chapter 5
Unseen Circumstances

"The Uninvited" was assumed to be a huge hit and money maker when it was released in 1944, but it was not even in the top twenty grossing movies for the year. By contrast, "The Lady in the Dark" was fourth for top grossing movies. Paramount did however, have four other films finishing in the top twenty.

While "The Uninvited" couldn't be considered a box office smash, or flop for that matter, it did gain notoriety as the best ghost movie in Hollywood history. This reputation dramatically increased when it was shown on television years later. Ruth Hussey, when asked if she, or anyone else from the cast and crew of "The Uninvited" knew they were making a classic replied, "No, I didn't think anybody did. This is from what I read too. We thought it would be a good movie…interesting and kind of different, with well mounted, gorgeous sets and a good cast. But as far as it being a classic and a big hit… I don't think it was a big hit at first, was it?" Then, when she was asked if it became a classic after it played on TV, she agreed it was by saying, "That's right."[1]

Elizabeth Russell downplayed her part in the movie, "I had no dialogue or billing, and you could hardly make me out on screen in the few seconds I had, but I made more money from it than I did from some of my larger roles. I play a much discussed ghost named Mary Meredith. Everyone thought in life she had been a saint, but in the end, she is revealed in all her true malevolence haunting this old house on the English coast. Prior to shooting I had to pose for a large portrait that was important to the story and was to be displayed in the film. It was painted by a charming Englishman named Kitchen. I went to his studio for about a week and was on payroll all that time. To say that my part in the movie wasn't much is an overstatement. I was to be seen barely floating down the staircase of this isolated seaside house. It took much longer to shoot than they expected…the main problem was getting me to float believably. I was suspended on wires. They wrapped me in some kind of gauze for the special effect they wanted, as a result I became stiff as a board. It took days to work it out, but they finally got the shot. People have told me the result on screen was very eerie and believable, though, and worth the trouble. Paramount said I could have the portrait, but it was so huge I didn't know how to get it home."[2] The portrait ended up hanging in a Los Angeles Museum.

Though it was a hardship to make the film, Gail with some insight declared, "At that time I WAS that girl in "The Uninvited," shy about meeting people. Except for the English accent, all I had to do was be myself. And that wall of eyes behind the camera is what gets me. Hundreds of eyes gleaming in the dark, staring at me, boring holes in me, giving me the heebies. Horrible, I worry, worry, and worry. In one month, I've lost six pounds worrying. I'm just going around in circles. Confusing is the word. I was very happy when they gave me the part."[3]

People who knew Gail agreed that the role of Stella Meredith couldn't have been acted by anyone better. She was Stella inside and out. Gail's reviews were generally good with adjectives like talented, beautiful, and youthful used to describe her. The Los Angeles Examiner reported, "Miss Russell is a newcomer and a real new star in the making if I ever saw one. This former Santa Monica High School girl is a fresh and unique personality. But more important, she is a splendid actress. Her handling of the difficult role of Stella Meredith is amazing-a finished performance of a tortured, haunted girl seeking maternal love from a ghost." Fans and critics alike enjoyed "The Uninvited" and agreed it was the best ghost story ever filmed.

Gail was sent to New York by Paramount to promote the film and meet with the brass. While there, she attended the premiere accompanied by Paramount executives. Gail hated everything about making films, but she detested more what Paramount expected of her after a movie was completed. The way the executives treated her as if she were a piece of property, to do with however they pleased. She also disliked all the noisy crowds and pushy reporters. After the premiere was over, Gail returned to the solitude of her hotel room, where she stayed for the remainder of her stay. She expressed no interest in seeing Broadway shows or tourist attractions. Moreover, she was completely despondent and swore never to attend another premiere.

At the start of filming "The Uninvited" Gail weighed 125 pounds (she stood 5'3"). After her return from New York, she was tipping the scale at 106. Her drop in weight was caused by a combination of events that were causing her to suffer a nervous breakdown.

Required to work much longer and harder hours in her first co-starring role was a tremendous burden. Fortifying herself with alcohol to get through the day's shoots, coupled with family issues was too much for the young actress. Seeing that there was a problem, the studio sent Gail to Phoenix, Arizona for a month to get her rested and ready for her next movie. The trip was kept under wraps by the studio. To keep Gail company, her friend Carmelita Lopez went with her. Carmelita's father was a cameraman for Twentieth Century Fox and Carmelita had occasional bit parts at Paramount. She was one of the few people Gail made friends with and became a confident of sorts. Gail would also stay with Carmelita when quarrels erupted in the Russell family.

What were the basis of these quarrels? Her parents fought often over their financial situation. But did they also fight over the continuation of a career that Gail didn't want? Or was there something else? It may be that her parents saw early clues of her drinking.

While Gail was in Arizona, Gladys hoped for Gail's return, saying, "I never left off doing for her in those days. I never let her know how desperate we were at losing her. I still mended her clothes when I had a chance, and despite her tears, I'd plant the seeds that I hoped would bring her back someday."

Gail reverted back to her old habits growing up in Chicago. She retreated to her room for days with her coffee, radio, and puzzles, sometimes sketching for hours, living the life of a solitary artist. In her room, Gail kept a collection of stuffed animals along with toy ones. She also had a little dog named "Hank" that kept her company.

After returning home from Arizona, Gail moved out of the family home into an apartment. "A family doesn't know or understand how hard it is to concentrate." Said Gail, from her small apartment in Beverly Hills.[4]

Her next film for Paramount was from another popular book turned into a movie. "Our Hearts Were Young and Gay."

Author Cornelius Otis Skinner along with best friend Emily Kimbrough traveled to Europe in their youth. A couple of college girls anxious to see the world. Skinner and Kimbrough helped write the screenplay with Sheridan Gibney then producer. Lewis Allen would be the director once more, having been given the project by Buddy DeSylva. Allen didn't think this constituted a big favor because it meant he would be working with Gail again. "Lew," said

DeSylva, amused "you can manage her. You did such a good job on 'The Uninvited' you're going to be stuck with Gail again."[5] Allen didn't find anything to be amused about. Having to cajole an emotionally disturbed girl once while making a movie was bad enough, much less twice.

Shooting for the movie commenced on August 18, 1943. When Charley Brackett visited the set he said, "I heard Lew fuming at Gail, whom he kicked out of 'Our Hearts were Young and Gay,' but readmitted after she wept and promised to be ameable."[6] Gail was understandably apprehensive. "At first, I wasn't crazy to do 'Our Hearts Were Young and Gay' it was based on the book by Cornelia Skinner and Emily Kimbrough about their misadventures in Europe during the 1920s. I felt inadequate to portray a distinguished woman like Miss Skinner. Even at that time I was still new to pictures and a little frightened of them yet. But my good friend Diana Lynn pushed me to do it with her. My acting coach William Russell also said, 'Grab it. You'll have fun.' But it is a wild and wooly comedy part and you must be prepared to make a damn fool of yourself."[7]

From a rough start, Gail gradually improved her on-set behavior. Allen credited her co-star Diana Lynn saying, "A very expressive girl who took Gail under her wing and coached her. They worked very well together, and I had no trouble with Gail on that picture. Thanks to Diana, Gail lost a lot of her inhibitions."[8] It may be conjecture, but Gail may have been losing her inhibitions because of another reason; daily travels to the café across from Paramount for a drink.

It had taken some time for Gail to warm up to Diana Lynn, or anybody else for that matter, but slowly they became friends. Together, Gail and Diana worked at the Hollywood Canteen, a place that offered food, dancing, and entertainment for servicemen, usually on their way overseas. A serviceman's ticket for admission was his uniform, and everything in the Canteen was free of charge. Gail even visited wounded soldiers recovering from injuries. It was a difficult experience for Gail, given her shy nature. But the appearance of a movie actress never failed to cheer up the soldiers.

Although Lynn was two-years younger than Gail, she was more like the older sister looking out for the youngest. As they say opposites attract and in the case of Diana and Gail it was true. Where Gail was shy, Dian was outgoing and enjoyed making friends. A child prodigy on the piano, she made her film debut in

1939. It was while on the set of "Henry Aldrich Gets Glamour" that the two had met and formed a friendship. Working together on "Our Hearts were Young and Gay" brought them even closer.

Gail made another friendship around this time with an actress named Yvonne De Carlo. Born in Canada, Yvonne was two-years older than Gail; while waiting for a big role, Yvonne was signed to Paramount as another Dorothy Lamour. She contradicted Allen about Gail's introduction to alcohol saying, "There was an actress on the lot who would show Gail how to cope, the good natured but tough talking Helen Walker. She took Gail under her wings and introduced her to the tranquilizing effects of Vodka."[9] Vodka is popular among drinkers because it has a reputation as being odorless and tasteless, which isn't really factual. The taste and smell of Vodka are just easier to cover up because it doesn't leave a strong smell on one's breath like other alcoholic beverages. Gail justified her drinking by saying that it relaxed her when acting in front of people and made her more sociable.

De Carlo saw up close the torment that Gail was going through at Paramount. "I felt that I had much in common with her, but she was much more vulnerable than I. She confided in a hushed tone how she wished her mother Gladys had never dragged her to Paramount for her screen test. She despised acting and everything it entailed, especially being put on display before executives and a film crew. I sympathized with her misery but I had no soothing words for her."[10] De Carlo got her big break in "Salome where She Danced" and starred in movies for over a decade. Today she is mostly remembered for Lily in the 1965 television series, "The Munsters."

Skinner and Kimbrough visited the set to see the two young actresses portraying them. Meeting Gail and Diana was pleasant but both ladies found themselves dazzled by the beauty of Miss Russell and Miss Lynn, "If I looked like them 20-years-ago I wouldn't have needed to go to Europe," said Emily. Cornelia agreed.[11]

The story of a couple of unsophisticated college girls touring Europe and Paris, getting themselves and others into mishaps is charming and delightful. After completing the movie, Gail was glad that she had taken the role, saying, "I gave in. The script had Diana and I doing everything; wearing money bags that dangled between our legs, wrapping ourselves in molting white fur coats, losing our clothes on top of Notre Dame Cathedral and getting measles. It turned out to be my happiest filmmaking experience and a big success, as well as my favorite movie." Miss Skinner was pleased too and wrote to Gail, "Dear Gail: Thanks so much for letting me see a copy of the story that's to be published by *Movieland Magazine.* It's most interesting and I like it very much. I attended a private showing of 'Our Hearts Were Young and Gay' and I think it's excellent and you're charming in it. I'm sorry I didn't see you when you were in New York, but when you come back again do get in touch with me. See you again. Affectionately, Cornelia."[12] Gail named her pet dog, a Maltese Terrier, Corny (after Cornelia) for good luck.

The movie was received by both critics and fans as wonderful and an enjoyable way to spend an afternoon in a theatre.

One duty that established stars have to partake in are interviews to writers that cover Hollywood in magazines and newspapers. The studios expect those under contract to promote the movie they appear in and give an envious picture of the glamorous life of a star. Gail obliged reluctantly and was never comfortable during these interviews. She was known to get up and walk away if the question was too probing. Still, she played the game when asked about being a movie star, saying, "It's been fun, but it's been a strain because all my old class mates ask me about life in a studio and how films are made. And I've got to sound very knowing. Like an authority after my first day when I saw a movie camera for the first time in my life. Nobody could have been greener. The first month was the hardest. I used to find myself going dramatic when on a dance floor and entering my room in the grand film manner. But I snapped out of all that. I hope." When asked what she wanted from making movies, she replied, "Enough money to quit and buy a ranch where I can keep a horse."[13]

Gail completed four movies so far, co-starring in two within the space of two-years. That's a fast rise to the top for anybody. It was that swift accent that amazed her; she hardly had time to catch her breath. But the visions of big money that stars made turned out to be an illusion. Gail received only a small increase in her weekly $50 dollar salary.

Her parents may have been pleased to have a daughter in the movies, but Gail wasn't. Gail's brother George, who was stationed in Alaska for the last two and a half years, had missed Gail's rise to fame. To prove to his buddies that his little sister was a movie queen, he had her send glamour shots that he handed out to the boys.

Gail found ways to handle the pressures of being a movie actress, "I knock myself out. Then I can't think about pictures. I'm too tired. I come to work on Mondays all black and blue from horseback riding. But it's brought me through another holiday and those are the worst days."[14]

Was Gail hoping to suffer a bad injury and be unable to report to work? Clearly, she was looking for a way out, an escape from the life she was caught up in. Breaking a leg would be a temporary solution. The other recourse was to break her contract. Others had done it. If it was just Gail alone, she may have summoned the strength to pursue such an option. But in her current situation, there were her parents, particularly her mother, who was seeing a long-ago dream come true.

Despite her trepidations, Gail's career continued to blossom. Her next movie "Salty O'Rourke" gave Gail a chance to work with Alan Ladd, a promising actor who was starting to have an impact and Raoul Walsh, an accomplished director. Walsh began as a stage actor in New York. In 1914, he started learning his craft under D.W. Griffin and eventually directed movies with Douglas Fairbanks. He also placed an unknown actor by the name of Marion Morrison in an early talkie called "The Big Trail" Morrison would later change his name and become famous the world over as John Wayne. A few years later, Wayne would have a major impact on Gail's life.

Alan Ladd rose to stardom in the years before Gail made her appearance in the movies. His break through role was in the film "This Gun for Hire," and starred Ladd as a hired killer. Before his movie career, Ladd was on the radio, getting small parts in movies. Now he was slowly becoming a bigger draw along with Veronica Lake and Bob Hope. Along with these emerging stars, Paramount still had Bing Crosby, Gary Cooper, and Dorothy Lamour.

Gail was well cast as the teacher, Miss Brooks; Ladd a gambler trying to hustle a young jockey to win races for him. In the movie, Gail convinces Ladd of the error of his ways and falls in love with him at the same time. Gail and Ladd worked well together. Not quite the on-screen chemistry he favored with Veronica Lake, but they were a good matchup nonetheless. Despite his image portraying tough guys, Ladd was insecure and as vulnerable as Gail. In addition, he carried quite a bit of emotional baggage and was sensitive about his height. Ladd felt that he had to prove himself time and time again in a world of giants. Additionally, both carried wounds concerning their mothers. Ladd feeling that he failed to rescue his mother from a life of poverty and alcohol.

Gail's brother George returned from Alaska around this time with the rank of Private First Class; his first furlough in two-years. On his first night home, Gail asked him where he would like to go. He chose the ice follies. Halfway through the show, Gail asked George the question that had been bothering her. After looking at snow and glaciers, how come you want to see ice when you get to Californian? "Why, I haven't even noticed the ice," grinned George. "I was watching those pretty girls."[15]

Most of Gail's co-stars noticed her unease when making films: the glazed look, unsteady footing, forgetting lines and wringing her hands constantly. One way to ease the tension on a film set and let off some steam was to play pranks or harmless jokes; so long as they didn't go too far. Sidney Lanfield had found out previously that Gail could be pushed too far. Even with the joking and pranks going on during filming, Gail was assailed with doubts about her love scene with Ladd, "So I decided," said Gail "that if I had to be the femme fatale I ought to see how the experts do it. I asked the studio to run off for me six of the hottest love scenes they could dig up. I spent six hours in the project room. The temperature got hotter with each reel but it was a very enlightening time." Gail watched stars Garbo, Valentino, and Shearer at their best. Two days later, Gail played her big love scene with Ladd. Later she remarked, "I've learned more about this kissing routine in the last sixty seconds than I did in six hours watching someone else do it. How about making a re-take?"[16]

The majority of the reviews for "Salty O'Rourke" were positive and the role of a teacher seemed to suit her. Bosley Crowther, the well-known movie critic for the New York Times, disagreed, saying, "Gail Russell doesn't quite play the teacher for all of its farce overtone, but that is because the director Raoul Walsh hasn't pitched the farce too well."[17] Mr. Crowther was of course in the minority about Gail's performance.

Paramount wanted to capture some of the noteworthy achievements of "The Uninvited," by again taking a popular novel and turning it into a successful movie. This time the novel in mind was "The Midnight House" penned by Ethel Lina White. Born in Wales in 1876 Ethel began writing as a child. In due course, she became recognized as one of the best crime writers in Britain and the United States. Her novel the "The Midnight House" was renamed in America to "Her Heart in Her Throat." When production for the movie began the working title became "Fear." Then finally it was changed to "The Unseen," making it easier for movie goers to connect with "The Uninvited."

"The Unseen" marked John Houseman's beginning as a producer. Born Jacques Hussmann in Romania, he worked as a grain trader in London before immigrating to America where he became an actor and took the stage name, John Housman. Lewis Allen took the helm as director and Script writing duties were given to Raymond Chandler. Chandler, who began writing after losing his job during the Great Depression, excelled at his work; his specialty being detective fiction. Unfortunately, Chandler garnered a reputation as an erratic drunk; up one moment, down the next, like a yo-yo.

If Allen expected the troublesome actress from the previous films they worked on together, he was surprised. "By the time I got around to 'The Unseen,' said Allen, "Gail was becoming quite professional."[18] The reason for the newfound professionalism? This was Gail's sixth movie, by now her confidence had grown with help from Diana Lynn and the occasional visit to the Paramount café. It also helped that Gail was working with top-notch actors, Joel McCrea and Herbert Marshall.

McCrea, since he was a boy wanted to be an actor. Raised in Pasadena, California, he delivered newspapers to famed director Cecil B. DeMille. Before he became a star he worked as an extra and a stunt man and anything else demanded of him. By the time "The Unseen" rolled around he had starred in two dozen films with Westerns being his specialty. Herbert Marshall was an English screen actor. During World War One he was seriously injured and had to have his leg amputated. During World War Two he visited handicapped soldiers and inspired them to overcome whatever disability they were facing. Marshall debuted in 1927, appearing in movies that showcased his charm and manners.

The plot of the movie centers on a murder that took place in Salem Alley, in New England, next door to the home of David Fielding (McCrea). Gail, playing Elizabeth Howard, is sent by the employment agency to fill the vacancy of governess for Fielding's two children, Barnaby, and Ellen. Fielding is a recent widower, having lost his wife in a suspicious car crash. At first, he is put off by Elizabeth, thinking her too young and inexperienced. However, after a discussion he decides to give Elizabeth a chance.

As the movie progresses, Elizabeth learns about the mystery of the boarded up house next door. The house was once owned by a man Fielding worked for, named Tygarth, whose murder went unsolved. His widow Marian has since moved out of the house but still lives in the neighborhood.

As Elizabeth settles in to her new surroundings, Ellen takes to her, but Barnaby is aloof and hostile and wants the former governess Maxine to come back. Elizabeth also starts to notice things that strike her as odd. Like when Barnaby hangs a stuffed animal in his window or answers phone calls then denies it.

Fielding introduces Elizabeth to Dr. Charles Evens (Herbert Marshall), the neighbor from across the street. She also meets a jumpy realtor named Jasper Goodwin, played by Norman Lloyd, who tries to talk Fielding into selling his house. And this is when things start to get creepy. Shortly after meeting Dr. Evan and Jasper, Ellen shows Elizabeth her scrap book that has a newspaper clipping of an unidentified woman murdered on Salem Alley. Shortly thereafter, Elizabeth finds a mysterious gold watch in one of Ellen's dresser drawers. Presenting it to Fielding, he pockets it.

The next evening, Marian Tygarth shows up, asking to use the phone to call a taxi. Elizabeth offers to make the call for her. Picking up the phone she overhears Barnaby talking. Confronting him later about the call, the boy is evasive. Later that evening, Elizabeth goes for a walk with Ellen and Barnaby and is talked into seeing a late movie. Leaving the theater at night, they become disoriented as to what streets to take to get home. Following Barnaby's directions, they find themselves in Salem Alley, where the woman from Ellen's scrapbook was found murdered. Glancing at the shadows on the buildings, Elizabeth and the children get spooked and make a mad dash for home. Bursting in the front door Fielding questions Elizabeth. After hearing what happened in Salem Alley, he becomes angry and reprimands her.

Strange things continue to go unexplained in the Fielding home. Barnaby having more money than his fifty cents a week allowance could explain and Mr. Fielding coming and going at odd hours. Furthermore, both children are secretive about the mysterious house next door and their former governess, Maxine.

One night, while Elizabeth is alone in the kitchen, a noise from the cellar startles her. Investigating, she finds Chester, the furnace worker. After he leaves, she returns to the kitchen and discovers several coins left on the condiment shelf. They are the same kind of coins that Barnaby keeps. A moment later, Elizabeth hears someone come in the front door and goes to investigate. She finds that Mr. Fielding has returned. She tells him about the odd things going on that night, but he discredits her. Elizabeth storms off full of indignation.

The next day's newspaper identifies the woman that was murdered on Salem Alley. Finding the children playing, Elizabeth inquires about the clipping in Ellen's scrapbook, only to find that it has been torn out. Elizabeth reprimands both children for not being truthful about the identity of the murdered woman.

Confiding her fears to Dr. Evans, he reassures Elizabeth that there is nothing to worry about and dissuades her from going to the police. Scared over the murder, Fielding's two housekeepers decide to leave. Not desiring to stay by herself with the children, Elizabeth contacts the employment agency and Ellen finally spills the beans as to how Barnaby earns extra money. She tells Elizabeth that Barnaby leaves a stuffed toy elephant hanging in his window to signal that the door is unlocked to gain entrance to the boarded up house by way of the cellar. A duty their former governess Maxine carried out. Elizabeth also learns that Barnaby witnessed the murder next door and retrieved the gold watch. Hearing this, Elizabeth rushes downstairs to bolt the door. As she leans against the door to catch her breath the knob twists back and forth. Dr. Evans is called over, but Mr. Fielding arrives first to find Elizabeth at his desk holding the gold watch that she gave to him earlier. Dr. Evan comes upon the scene puzzled, but leaves since his services are not needed. When Fielding questions Elizabeth she breaks away, pleading to be left alone. Detective Sullivan calls on Fielding when informed that he has the watch, but Fielding denies it and assumes it was Elizabeth who called the police.

Early the next morning, a woman arrives, applying for the position of housekeeper. Barnaby is extremely happy to see her, swearing Ellen to silence. Introducing herself as Mary, she is hired and shown her room. When Fielding arrives home, Elizabeth meets him and denies that she called the police. Their conversation is interrupted by a phone call from the employment agency, letting them know that the new housekeeper is due tomorrow. Elizabeth then realizes that Mary and Maxine are the same person.

Barnaby, meanwhile, is in Maxine's room giving a narrative of the murder on Salem Alley. Mr. Fielding comes in the room, orders Barnaby away and tells Maxine (Mary) to leave the premises. As she leaves, she runs into Barnaby. He pleads with her not to leave, making her mad enough to strike him, Elizabeth enters the scene and comforts the hurt boy. She then runs downstairs in pursuit of Maxine only to find her across the street, dead. She then runs frantically to Dr. Evans residence screaming for help.

The police, with Dr. Evan in tow, inspect the crime scene. Marian Tygarth comes to console Elizabeth, while Barnaby decides to go to the boarded house and return the money that he was paid for leaving the door open. Talking with Elizabeth, Marian divulges the truth about her husband's murder and that the man responsible is in the house now, ensuring that he left no clues behind before it is reopened. As Marian leaves, she tells Elizabeth to keep playing the piano, a signal to the killer that the coast is clear. In the meantime, Ellen has become restless, and tells Elizabeth that Barnaby is planning on going into the house to return the money. Frantic, Elizabeth rushes to the boarded up house to head him off.

When she gets there, she finds that Marian is already there to reveal the true identity of her husband's murderer, a former lover. In the process, Marian is fatally shot. Elizabeth and Barnaby hear the gun fire and flee back to the safety of their home.

Once back at home, it is revealed that Mr. Fielding was at the house as well and overheard Dr. Evans and Marian talking just before Dr. Evans killed her. He notifies the police and they quickly take Dr. Evans into custody. After going through such a nightmare ordeal, Elizabeth and Mr. Fielding realize how much they care for each other. They decide to leave with the children and begin a new life.

With such a confused storyline it's no wonder "The Unseen" failed to reach the heights that "The Uninvited" attained. A case of too many hands in the pot. Director Allen reported that there was trouble between scriptwriter Chandler and producer, John Houseman. "Raymond had problems with John," said Allen. "Houseman was sitting there with a pencil going over the script and making notes. Raymond got up and took the script and threw it into the waste basket and said, 'look, I'm the f***ing writer on this picture, not you.' He was writing the script and Houseman was always interfering; wanting to change this and that. I was on Chandler's side. I said look John, Ray's a very good writer, let's trust him."[18]

With Chandler, Hagar Wild and Houseman all contributing to the script, its little wonder the story is confusing.

Paramount clearly was hoping to duplicate the success of "The Uninvited." With a similar title, fans came out expecting a sequel where the previous movie ended, with Stella and Rick going off into another spooky adventure. One of the things that disappointed fans was that "The Unseen" didn't deal with the supernatural, like "The Uninvited" did. Another problem was that the murderer turns out to be the kindly Dr. Evans, who must have been pretty spry to run from one place to the other, never out of breath.

Herbert Marshall and Joel McCrea are fine actors, but were hampered by a garbled script. Norman Lloyd broke up the heavy handed story with a couple of comical turns as Goodwin the realtor. Gail got more screen-time than she had ever had up to this point in her career, and was given more scenes to showcase her growing abilities. She also worked well with the child actors.

However, there were scenes where Gail is constantly wringing and clinching her hands, showing that she still had issues with nervousness. It was a habit that she fought to break. Gail's wardrobe is fashionable, showcasing different assortments of dresses with cuffs and collars. The costume designer was not the well-known Edith Head who worked on "The Uninvited" but Dorothy O'Hara. Gail wore clothes like a top flight fashion model, but had no interest in them herself. She liked slacks and sweaters, simple blouses, and skirts. And since childhood, she insisted her clothes be plain so she wouldn't be noticed.

In several scenes Gail reverted to her old habit of dropping her head. And one scene is ironic. Mr. Fielding offers Elizabeth a drink which she refuses, saying she doesn't drink. As far as actual drinking on the set went, there was no reported problems; if Gail was drinking, she kept it under wraps. Norman Lloyd said, "I saw no signs of alcohol at the time. I can't give you anything on Gail because she was rather remote-in a nice way."[21]

Reviews of Gail's performance were mixed. "As the governess, busily straightening out the children, falling in love with the father and unraveling the mystery, she's not really masterful enough or sufficiently sure of herself. But as a girl who looks the way you feel when you're sure there's something in the next room, Miss Russell is right on."[19]

Gail looked back with fondness on both of the films: "I liked to play in those spooky stories. It was the ghosties that gave me my break. Going from 'The Uninvited' to 'The Unseen' yes, that was really frightening," she exclaimed. "And after that I was put, still trembling, into a horror drama." She laughed as she talked about them, an easy laugh, even while looking like a startled fawn. And she is an Edger Allen Poe fan. "After Poe," says Gail "most horror yarns fall flat. They may be fun, but not really frightening. I don't read mysteries either, none except Poe's. After the victim is killed, I lose interest in him."[20] (When Gail lived in Chicago as a child her father would come home from playing in a local orchestra late at night. He would knock on her door and the two would head for the ice box. Once there they would talk about music, art, and poetry. Being that Poe was her favorite poet, Gail would recite the Raven.)

After "The Unseen" Gail became a full-fledged movie star, much to the amazement to those who knew her. When asked if he was surprised, director Allen laughed, and said, "Very." Gladys said, "It is difficult for me to understand how it is possible for Gail to become an actress."[22] This coming from the woman who dragged her reluctant daughter to the studio in the first place. Watching from the sidelines as Gail's film career was soaring, photographed, and written about in magazines, Gladys no doubt thought that it could have been her.

But there was a price that Gail was paying for stardom. Hollywood gossip columnist, Louella Parsons invited Gail to her home for an Interview. "I was amazed when I talked to her to see how much weight she had lost, and how she had changed from the plump little girl. She weighs 105 now and I thought at first, she was unhappy. Her smile came so rarely and the day she came to my house she seemed to have something on her mind. Finally, she told me." "I've been so sick," she said. "For the first time in my life I get dizzy and faint; sort of lose my equilibrium."

"I started to tell her what to do. Then I stopped."

"Go on," she said, "what else shall I do?"

"I told her, go to the head of your studio, and tell them to recommend a good doctor. Hearing that Gail replied, "I wanted to be an artist, I still do. But my mother wanted either my brother or myself to go into the movies. When I told her I'd been sent for to make a screen test she was dressed in a minute flat to take me to the studio. I guess it was fate. I got the job because, when a note came from the studio, I thought it was some of the kids fooling and I threw the note away, until a teacher told me it wasn't a joke."

After the interview, Parsons was concerned about Gail, commenting: "I'd like to have talked to her when she hadn't had something on her mind. She was so quiet it worried me. The only thing that interested her was a map of Ireland I had with the names of leading families. She looked up the name of Russell and was delighted to find it twice. "North or south of Ireland? I asked."

"North," she replied.[23]

Despite all that Gail had accomplished and suffered through, she still held onto the dream of becoming an artist. It was now time for happy times; something she was overdue for.

In 1945 Gail met a good looking young man by the name of Guy Madison, who recently moved into an apartment next door. Although not attracted to Guy at first, he slowly grew on the young actress. But at this time, Gail still kept mostly to herself painting with oils during her off hours and occasionally creating clay models. Gail also spent a lot of time doing crossword puzzles and was a voracious reader, sometimes as many as five books a week. However, her health habits weren't the best. She usually ate a meal at night, drank coffee non-stop and smoked frequently. When she got bored of reading or doing crossword puzzles, she would sometimes go for a walk. As a little girl in Chicago, she delighted in walking in the rain, something she could only occasionally do in sunny California. Once when Gail was asked by Hollywood writer Bob Thomas what Santa should bring to Hollywood, she replied, "Rain."

(Gail stated the year before she met Guy: "I have never been in love. I don't want to be in love. I don't want to get married for a long time. I have too much to do. I have a lot of people to repay for all they have done for me.")

More good things came Gail's way when her longtime drama coach, William Russell, was given his first chance at directing the movie "Our Hearts Were Grown Up," a sequel to the earlier film, "Our Hearts Were Young and Gay." William called Gail up with the news. "When I called to say I was directing 'Our Hearts Were

Grown Up,' she actually cried. She's sincere. And I'm not giving you Hollywood baloney."[24]

Returning to the roles of Cornelia and Emily, this time Gail and Diana Lynn get involved with bootleggers in the roaring 1920's with prohibition in full force. Sneaking off to see a college football game with their boyfriends, the girls entice Mr. Minnetti to pose as their chaperone, little do they know what he does for a living. The bootleggers conceal the booze in the girl's luggage to hide it from the law. Upon discovering the bottles, the girls drain the alcohol and substitute it with a homemade concoction that gets served at a fancy dinner party. The girls then panic, fearing that they have poisoned everyone, but the brew is harmless. Cornelia and Emily are relieved and learn a valuable lesson about not to deceive.

It was during the filming of the movie that an eight-year-old boy named Ron Stephenson met Gail. Ron's father, an employee of Paramount, arranged a pass for Ron to visit during filming, even though it was a closed set. Most of Gail's sets were closed as a way to combat her stage fright. Years later, Ron remembered the atmosphere of the occasion saying, "Diana Lynn and the others actors were enjoying themselves, but when I was introduced to Gail, she was the opposite. Although not unpleasant, Gail avoided eye contact looking at the floor." That first meeting with Gail made a strong impression on Ron and turned him into a lifelong admirer. He kept up with the high and low points of Gail's career for the rest of her life.[25]

In time, Ron would become a well-known casting director. His credits include such hit shows as: "Murder She Wrote," "Columbo," "Simon and Simon" and "The Incredible Hulk."

Although "Our Hearts Were Grown Up" was not as well received as "Our Hearts Were Young and Gay," it stood on its own as a very amusing light-hearted movie.

Studios often loan out actors to other studios when they have nothing planed for them. The other studio pays their salary plus a bonus that goes directly to the actor's home studio. The actor or actress never sees a dime of it. It was the same with personal appearances. A fee was paid to the studio, but the actor only collected his or her regular weekly salary; it was a great deal for the studio. Some stars such as Bette Davis and others fought the studio system, but you had to be a big star to stand up to the power brokers of the studios. Gail's salary was increased as her career progressed, but she never made what a "Star" merited. For her next film, Gail would be on loan to United Artists.

"The Bachelor's Daughter" was Gail's next film and had a plot that had been seen before in movies. Gail is one of four girls' hoping to land a rich husband. She and the other girls persuade a floor walker in the department store where they work to pose as their father. Renting a mansion, Eileen (Gail) along with the others girls put up a charade of being wealthy. To play the part of a rich girl, Gail shop lifts high priced clothing from the department store, hoping to impress a boy she met. She then gets caught trying to return the stolen clothes. In her shame and fear she overdoses on sleeping pills. In the nick of time Gail is rescued and all ends happy for everyone. The girls admit the farce and go off with the men of their dreams.

The film is charming to watch and was well received. It was also one of the first films ever to be released to television in the 1950's. Joining Gail in the cast was Adlophe Menjou, Jane Wyatt, Ann Dvorack and Claire Trevor. Trevor's memory of Gail is pretty much what others have said, "Beautiful, but a loner."[26]

Feeling tired and spent, Gail needed a breath of fresh air. She would get it in her next movie, meeting the man who would become her champion in the process.

Chapter 6
Quirt and Penelope

Traveling to Sedona, Arizona to make a movie on location was a new experience for Gail. Her previous movies had all been shot on a sound stage in Hollywood. "Angel and the Badman" would be Gail's tenth movie. Arriving in Sedona was a thrill for the artist in Gail. The landscape was magnificent, with red sandstone formations covering the desert scenery. And when the sun set, the formations glowed a brilliant orange and red. Since the early days of silent movies, Sedona was used as a movie location. Besides Sedona, principal photography took place in Flagstaff and Monument Valley, Utah.

Gail grew anxious to meet John Wayne, or, "The Duke," as everyone called him. Would he be a gentleman like her drama coach, William Russell, or a lout like Sidney Lanfield?

In short time, Gail found out what kind of a man John Wayne was. There has been a lot said about "The Duke." There are those who praised him and those who ridiculed everything he stood for.

Born Marion Mitchell Morrison on May 26, 1907 his movie career began in the 1920s playing small bit parts. During this time Marion paid his dues working up from low budget, poverty row pictures to top flight movies. In 1930, Marion got his big break: a leading role in a western called "The Big Trail." Along with the movie came a name change. With the rugged masculinity that western movies projected, the name Marion would never do; so, John Wayne was born. He would go on to star in 142 movies and become one of the most famous and recognizable movie icons of all time.

As Gail and John began working together, Wayne recognized Gail's anxiety and insecurities, but he was kind and patient with her. He may have been feeling a little insecure himself. "Angel and the Badman" launched Wayne's first attempt at production and he had just recently signed a new contract with Republic Studios. The deal gave him a free hand in picking his next film, casting, and hiring actors and editing films to his liking.

Starting his first production, "The Duke" wanted to make sure he had the best people assisting him. One of the first people Wayne hired was Mary St. John. Mary was in charge of the secretarial pool at Republic and had been with the studio since 1936. After Wayne scored big with the movie "Stagecoach" he told her if he ever needed an assistant, he'd want her. In 1946 as "Angel and the Badman" began to take fruition she accepted the job. The next person "The Duke" hired was James Grant. Grant was a former Chicago newspaperman. After moving to the west coast, he became a successful screenwriter. Wayne had known him since the early 1940s and they became drinking buddies. It was Grant who wrote a script entitled "The Angel and the Outlaw." Its basic plot was about a gunfighter who falls in love with a Quaker girl hoping to reform him. It was a tad different than the other westerns "The Duke" had done, but he liked the way Grant wrote and this was no different.

Grant though, wanted a chance at directing. Wayne pondered it and figured it was his first effort at producing, so why not give his pal a chance at directing. Wayne and Grant jumped into the making of the movie anxious to make good. They worked together like eager beavers at Wayne's home on the screenplay.

In hiring the crew, Wayne gave parts to people he had worked with before. Yakima Canutt was given the job as stunt coordinator. Canutt had started in silent movies and eventually starred in several. He later worked with Wayne, doubling him in his early roles. Canutt became one of the top stunt directors in Hollywood and was the man behind the famous chariot race in "Ben Hur." To this day rumors still persist that a man was killed during filming of the race. The truth is, it was in fact a well-constructed mechanical model that was crushed under the horse's hoofs. Archie Stout was hired as the cinematographer. Like Canutt, Stout began with Wayne early in his career.

Next came the job of picking the cast. Wayne gave roles to his friends Harry Carey and Bruce Cabot. Irene Rich was cast as the mother of the Quaker girl Penelope. Next came the major decision of the actress to play the role of the Quaker girl. Wayne didn't like any of the actresses Republic had available, so he contacted Paramount and paid $125,000 for the services of Gail Russell. Gail, at this time, was making $125.00 a week. Wayne tried to get Gail some of the loan-out money, but those "Pricks" over at Paramount wouldn't give her any.[1] Not a bad profit for Paramount.

Catalina Lawrence, the script supervisor for the film, recalled that Gail had talent to go along with her beauty saying, "She was just so beautiful. No one, not even Elizabeth Taylor, was as beautiful as Gail."[2]

Wayne was finding that being a producer was as demanding as being an actor. Making sure the schedule and everything connected with the film ran smoothly was a challenge. At times, he would explode if it didn't; he had a lot riding on this film.

Gail found it demanding also. Shooting outdoors was a different process than shooting on a sound stage and the environment takes direction from no one. Neither does an airplane flying overhead. It's an uncontrollable situation for everyone. The sun was another challenge. During shooting, it provides most of the light, so a cloud rolling by can ruin a shot.

During the filming, Gail was called upon to do some of her own stunts, although most of the time she was doubled. Here she gives first hand insight into filming in an outdoor environment. "None of which I've ever done in my life. In fact, the whole great outdoors was new to me. When Paramount told me they were loaning me out for a cowboy movie, I just blinked. Up to now I've done my acting indoors. But I can ride a horse. So, I figured it wouldn't be too awful," she chuckled.

Driving a four-wheeled buckboard though, was completely new to her. "I always thought they kind of took it easy on you the first day. But oh no! In my first scene, I had to drive that pesky thing from 6 O'clock in the morning until the light faded." After the first day, Gail was so bruised and sore she had to be helped off the buckboard. "After that I managed to tumble off myself. Either that or one of those sandstorms blew me off. And let me tell you about the heat. It was so hot out there the makeup man had to give all the actresses a completely new face every few hours; the original ones just melted off. Living with that chummy little herd of cattle was nice too. There's even a stampede in the picture, but for some strange reason I'm not down there under the hooves. Guess it never occurred to'em. I sure would have been."[3] No matter how grueling Gail made it sound, she was having the time of her life.

If Gail was taken by surprise at how a movie was filmed on location, she was more surprised by her co-star John Wayne. She expected to find something portrayed off a screen, like a rough and tough uneducated cowpoke. But instead, she found an intelligent and chivalrous man that she could talk to and confide in. And what surprised her most of all was the fact that he didn't make advances towards her as so many others in Hollywood had. "The Duke" had his flings, but he never took advantage of any young troubled girls like Gail. Years later, Wayne revealed what Gail had gone through at Paramount. "Gail was such a beautiful young girl that some of the SOB's at the studio had taken advantage of her. You know about the old casting couch? She'd been there a number of times. Well, it didn't happen with me."[4]

For Gail to reveal this about herself demonstrates how much she trusted Wayne. "In those days," said Bernu Acquanetta star of Tarzan and the Leopard women, "all a man in Hollywood would have to do is meet a woman and bang, he would come on to her. It was so common. I resented that to a degree. It makes me emotional now, because I would have liked to have stayed and made more pictures. But when I thought what one had to do for that, I walked away. That stops a lot of careers in and out of Hollywood, I must say."[5]

1950's actress Merry Anders, among others, concurred saying, "There were times in the industry when it was very seedy and very difficult. You had your share of being chased around a desk and everything else on auditions. You had to learn how to handle it. It wasn't easy because the producers and directors were doing the chasing and if they didn't like being rejected, they didn't hire you anymore."[6] Anders found one solution to the problem by having her mother accompany her. Diana Lynn's mother chaperoned her around the studio, but Gail didn't have that luxury.

Audrey Totter an actress in the same era as Gail refuted those tales of the casting couch. "I never ran into anybody who wasn't a nice guy. I don't know what they're like today, but they were all gentleman; they treated you like a lady. My story is I didn't sleep with anybody-nobody asked me. Nobody made any passes at you; nothing like that went on. There's this reputation out there that everybody's jumping in the hay. And with the movies you see today, you could believe it. I was under contract with MGM when L.B. Mayer ran the studio with an iron hand, and you better not make a pass at any of the actresses! I'm not saying that something like that didn't go on; I'm sure there were love affairs. But as someone being gross, coming on to you-no way!"[7]

This may be true, but Totter didn't look like Gail, and she wasn't under contract to Paramount. Shirley Temple in an interview told of producer Arthur Freed exposing himself to her as a 12-year-old girl and at the same time L.B. Mayer coming on to her mother. So much for ruling MGM with an iron hand.

Since the early days, Paramount had a bad reputation. The moguls sexually abused young actresses on a regular bases. Girls who played along were rewarded with parts in films or expensive gifts. "They'll never get me on the casting couch,"[8] said Thelma Todd. Thelma was loaned out by Paramount and then dropped. This was the environment that a scared teenage girl named Gail Russell found herself in, during 1943.

Who were the SOB's that Gail revealed to Wayne? He never did say. "I felt all she needed," said Wayne, "was someone to show her some kindness. She didn't understand it at all because she thought that I was like everyone else and wanted to take advantage of her. I didn't have to do or say anything specific to show her she was wrong. I just did what I could to encourage her and give her advice. But I never made any sexual advances on her and that took her by surprise. I advised her to say no to some of this crap."[9]

It was the behind the scene abuse that went on that may have helped contributed to Gail's drinking. It's not hard to imagine her drinking as a way to forget.

During filming of "Angel and the Badman" Gail fell for Wayne, something those around him noticed. Jimmy Grant mentioned it to "The Duke" saying, "You know she's got a real crush on you, don't you?" Wayne replied, "Yeah, but that's because she's not used to someone she's working for showing her real respect and kindness. I made sure Gail knew I wasn't like that. But when she wanted to talk, when she needed a friendly ear, I made sure I was there for her."[10]

Previously Jimmy Lydon, Ray Milland and Alan Ladd had all shown kindness and understanding to Gail. But the key word Wayne used is, "worked for." Milland, Ladd, and Lydon had worked with her. Nevertheless, rumors started to go around of an affair between Gail and "The Duke." Wayne's two sons, Mike, and Pat, who spent the summer on location during filming, always denied the rumors. "He felt sorry for her, she was really beautiful."[11] In fact, Wayne felt so bad for her that he and Grant chipped in for a down payment on a car for Gail. Another factor in Wayne's decision to not engage in an affair was the temperament of his wife, Chata. She could explode like a volcano. Seeing Gail and her husband together started fireworks. "Chata got so jealous anytime Gail even came towards his office Wayne would head out the back door," said Mary St. John.[12] Wayne later told Mary to, "Set Gail straight. Make sure she understands how I feel, but do it gently. The poor kids having a rough time."[13]

Guy Madison, the actor that Gail had been seeing off and on, visited her on the set and helped take her mind off of Wayne temporarily.

How much of the film Grant directed and how much Wayne did is debatable. Most agree that "The Duke" supervise how it was to be shot, while Grant directed scenes with Wayne's guidance and suggestions.

Finally, after the picture was finishing up Wayne could relax. A few days later the cast and crew had a wrap party to celebrate. Afterwards "The Duke" drove Gail home. Inebriated, Wayne talked to Gail's mother and her brother George as he tried to sober up for the drive home. Seeing that Wayne was still too drunk to drive after his visit, Gail called a taxi to take him home. Chata was awakened by his entry and exploded, almost shooting him in the process.

After surviving the near shooting, John looked forward to the release of the "Angel and the Badman." And as a first-time producer, he was anxious for fans and critics reactions to the film. Seeing his name on the screen as "John Wayne Productions" gave "The Duke" tremendous satisfaction.

The film starts with Quirt (Wayne) on the run and wounded. Penelope (Gail) and her father spot him just as he collapses off his horse. Gail's entrance is a grand one as she drives up in the buckboard and raises herself to full height. She eyes Quirt with no fear and he gives her the once over. Loading him in the buckboard Gail and her father drive him to the nearest telegraph office, where they discover he is a well-known gunfighter named Quirt Evans. Collapsing from his wounds, Gail and her father take him home and nurse him back to health over the next couple of weeks.

When Quirt first gains consciousness, he awakens startling Penelope. Questioning her, he discovers that she and her family are Quakers. She then tries to explain the Quaker faith to him. During her explanation, the local doctor who had been attending to Quirt warns the family to get rid of him because he is a dangerous gun fighter. In the meantime, four strangers led by a man named Laredo show up in town looking for Quirt. Informed of this, Quirt starts to take off, but Penelope confesses her growing feelings to him. A short time later, Laredo and his men show up at Penelope's house and Wayne greets them with drawn gun in hand. It's a tense scene, but all Laredo wants is the deed to Quirt's land, but his offer is to low and Quirt holds out for more.

After Laredo and his men leave, Quirt decides it's time to go but Penelope pleads with him to stay. Feeling perhaps he owes the Worths for their hospitality, he decides to stay a while and help out on the farm.

Quirt soon learns that Penelope and her family are having trouble with a neighboring rancher named Carson. The neighbor has damned up a stream that used to run through the Worths land. Paying the rancher a visit, Carson relents after discovering Quirts identity and has the damn busted open. Later, the territorial Marshall named McClintock stops by asking about Quirt and Penelope covers for him. Quirt soon appears and reassuring her that he and the Marshall go a long way back. After the Marshall rides off, Quirt joins Penelope and her family at a Quaker picnic.

On the way to the picnic they run into Randy, a friend of Quirt's who accepts the invitation to ride along with them. While at the picnic, Quirt is presented with a bible as a token for helping out and learns from his friend that Laredo plans to rustle a herd of cattle. With the help of Randy, Quirt thwarts the rustlers. Afterwards, Quirts celebrates in town but feels guilty about leaving Penelope and her folks. The next day, Quirt rides back to an over-joyed Penelope. Shortly thereafter, Marshall McClintock rides up to question Quirt about the rustlers. Quirt tells the Marshall that he wasn't involved and that one of the show girls back in town can verify his alibi. Suspicious, the Marshall warns Quirt that he will hang him some day.

Later that day, Quirt and Penelope go picking black berries and Quirt proposes to Penelope. Moments later, the two are ambushed by Laredo and his men. Unarmed, Wayne and Penelope have no choice but to flee in the buckboard. During the fast chase, Quirt and Penelope plunge over a cliff to the river below. Quirt manages to swim to shore with Penelope, but she is unconscious and injured. Enraged, Quirt heads for town to shoot it out with Laredo. Not long after he goes, Penelope regains consciousness, and she and her family ride to stop Quirt. Getting into town in the nick of time, Penelope gazes lovingly into Quirt's eyes, and he surrenders his gun to her. But just then, Laredo and his side-kick appear aiming to gun

Quirt down. Unarmed, Quirt turns and faces Laredo just in time to see Marshall McClintock gun down Laredo and his henchman. After a talk with the Marshall, Quirt swears off the outlaw lifestyle, saying he is now a farmer, and he and Penelope ride off toward the Worth homestead.

Viewing the movie today, people have different reactions. Some brush it off as corny saying, "Glad they don't make movies like that anymore." The names of the characters provoke laughter and the dialog is cliché ridden throughout the film. Then there are others who wish that Hollywood still made movies like it today. Good strong principals and strong characters that are well defined.

Regardless of the viewpoints taken, "Angel and the Badman" showcased the talents of Wayne and Russell for the first time, but not the last. Their chemistry captured everyone's attention, with some Wayne fans claiming it was the best of all.

When released, the movie was similar to the other films that Gail starred in; it wasn't listed in the top twenty movies of that year. Although not a great box office success, it did well enough. And like her performance in "The Uninvited," Gail earned terrific reviews. "Gail Russell is the lushly, lovely Quaker lass in whose goodness our hero becomes entangled like a fly in molasses. She doesn't gum it all up, in fact she presents the credo of the friends in a manner which would interest even the most cynical."[14]

The film's cinematography, done by Archie Stout, was superb. And his long range shots of the desert rock formations in the background are breathtaking to behold.

Reviewers and movie goers also noticed the way Gail looked at Wayne in their scenes; like a girl really enthralled with the leading man. What they didn't realize was that it came across so realistic because that's how Gail really felt.

Today "Angel and the Badman" is the movie that Gail Russell is best remembered for.

Gail at about three-years-old. Author's collection.

Gladys and Gail.

Gail's birth certificate showing the 1924 birth date and her birth name: Betty Gale Russell. Author's collection.

Gail, George Sr., Guy, and Gail's dog Kelly. Courtesy of Charlie Timmons.

Gail, George Sr., Gail's aunt Ruth Emma, and George Jr. Courtesy of Charlie Timmons.

Mary Stella (Gail's cousin) in Gail's Hollywood dress, 1961.

Gail's cousin Mary Stella (Midge). Note the resemblance to Gail. This is how Gail may have looked in her later years. Gail's end table is next to Mary. Courtesy of Charlie Timmons.

Gail with her father George. Courtesy of Ron Stephenson.

Gail on the left, Mary Stella (Midge) making a face and Aunt Suella sitting. Gail was in high school when this picture was taken. Reports that Gail never wore makeup before her movie career appear to be untrue. Courtesy of Charlie Timmons.

George, Gail, and Gladys. Author's collection.

Gail and her mother Gladys, 1947. Author's collection

The mother who wanted to be an actress with the daughter who became one. Courtesy of Ron Stephenson.

Gail with her mother Gladys. Author's collection.

Gail with Nona Griffith from the movie "The Unseen," 1945. Author's collection.

MOVIE LIFE OF GAIL RUSSELL *Continued*

1. GAIL RUSSELL was 18 months old in the above photograph. She's the daughter of the George H. Russells and was born in Chicago, September 21, 1925.

2. LAKE MICHIGAN—when she was three—with her mother, Gladys (holding Gail), and her Aunt Maude. Then, as now, Gail was shy, a problem, and a challenge.

3. BROTHER GEORGE, age seven, and Gail, now four years old, had this picture taken with their mother, after church, in front of their Chicago home.

4. RUSSELL FAMILY COMPLETE: George Russell, Gail's father, an insurance salesman; brother George; mother Gladys and Gail (standing timidly in the background) now seven. Photo was taken in backyard of home in Chicago's Hyde Park.

5. KOSMINSKI GRAMMAR SCHOOL, Chicago, grades 4A-4B. Gail is eighth from the left, third row. School was a trial since it involved constant association with many kids, and an inconspicuous dress was a *must* if she went to a party.

6. NOW 12, Gail posed here with her father in front of the Edgewater Beach Hotel in Chicago. She'd taken up art as a means of escape from social contacts.

7. ROLLER SKATING was one of her sports. Aside from her painfully shy reserve, Gail had the usual child's interest in strenuous athletic activities.

8. GLENDALE, CALIFORNIA, was next stop for the Russells. From there they moved to Santa Monica. Above, Gail (now 14) and mother snapped in California.

The photo left of center. Note how Gail is standing away from her family. Author's collection.

From Gail's 1941 University high school year book. Gail top row, second from end. Author's collection.

Gail top row, second from end. 1941 University high school. Author's collection.

Gail top row, third from end. 1941 University high school. Author's collection.

Gail's 1941 University high school year book showing a good example of her art work. Author's collection.

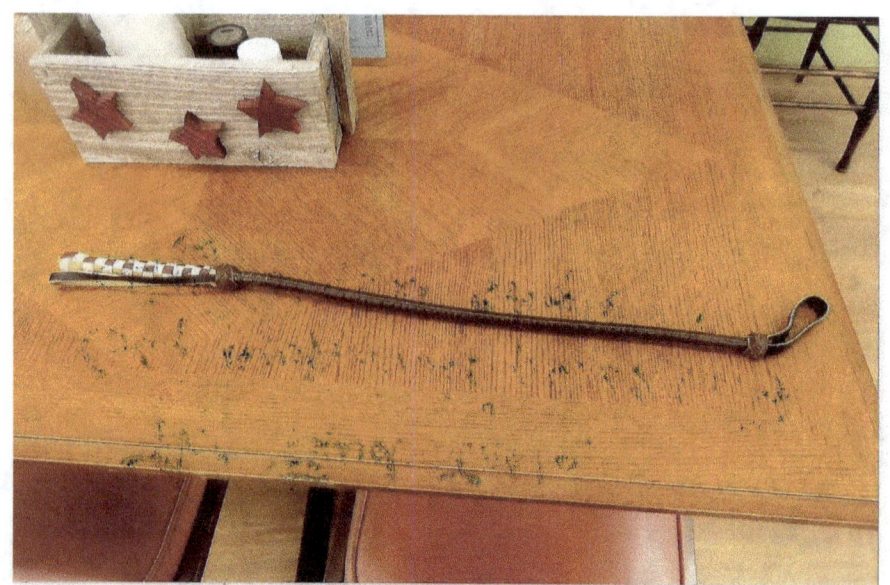
Gail's riding crop. Courtesy of Charlie Timmons.

Gail's long bow and end table. Courtesy of Charlie Timmons.

Gail's longbow "Little Sister." Courtesy of Charlie Timmons.

Charlie Timmons and his dad Joe. Joe is proudly wearing the cowboy hat Guy Madison gave to him, 1950. Author's collection.

Gail's painting of John Wayne and herself. This is the first time in over 50-years this painting has been seen by the public. Upper left hand corner Gail started a sketch of Harry Carey and Teddy Roosevelt. Courtesy of Charlie Timmons.

A rare clip of Gail drawing. Author's collection.

Gail reading at home. Author's collection.

Gail at home sketching. Author's collection.

The nose is right, but Gail isn't satisfied with the rest of her efforts at sculpting 'Guy. Once she's perfected the clay model, she'll make a bust of him. Gail's also interested in wood-carving, ceramics.

Gail and her dog Corny, 1945.
Author's collection.

From the movie "The Unseen," 1945. Gail, Nona Griffith, and Richard Lyon. Author's collection.

From the movie "The Great Dan Patch," 1949. Gail always looked forward to working with animals. Author's collection.

Gail and Lizabeth Scott with football star Johnny Lujack. Author's collection.

From the movie "Captain China," 1950. Jeffrey Lynn, John Payne, and Gail. Author's collection.

Gail faints in the movie "The Tattered Dress," 1957.
Courtesy of Ron Stephenson.

Macdonald Carey and Gail. From the movie "The Lawless," 1950.
Courtesy of Ron Stephenson.

John Lund, Gail, and Edward G. Robinson. From the movie "Night has a Thousand Eyes," 1948. Courtesy of Ron Stephenson.

Gail sporting a new hair style in the movie "Air Cadet," 1951. Courtesy of Ron Stephenson

Alan Ladd and Gail Russell. From the movie "Calcutta," 1947. Courtesy of Ron Stephenson.

Joel McCrea and Gail. From the movie "The Unseen," 1945. Courtesy Ron Stephenson.

Gail comforts a migrant worker in the movie "The Lawless," 1950. Courtesy of Ron Stephenson.

Sabu, Gail, and Turhan Bey. From the movie "Song of India," 1949. Courtesy of Ron Stephenson

Macdonald Carey and Gail Russell. From the movie "The Lawless," 1950. Courtesy of Ron Stephenson.

Dane Clark and Gail dance in the movie "Moonrise," 1948. Courtesy Ron Stephenson.

John Wayne and Gail Russell. From the movie "Angel and the Badman," 1947. Wayne protecting Gail. A role he played for real.
Courtesy of Ron Stephenson.

"The Duke" and Gail. From the movie "Wake of the Red Witch," 1948. Courtesy of Ron Stephenson.

Wayne and Gail. From the movie "Angel and the Badman," 1947. Penelope reforms the gunman Quirt. Courtesy Ron Stephenson.

Gail and "The Duke" in "Wake of the Red Witch." 1948.
Courtesy of Ron Stephenson.

Gail and "The Duke." From the movie "Wake of the Red Witch 1948. Angelique confronts Captain Rawls after his near death struggle with the Octopus. Author's collection.

Gail and Ray Milland. From the movie "The Uninvited."
Courtesy of Tom Weaver

John Payne and Gail Russell. From the movie "El Paso."
Courtesy of Ron Stephenson.

Gail Russell watches Lee Marvin twirls his six guns. From the movie "Seven Men from Now," 1956. Courtesy of Ron Stephenson.

Gail, John Lund, and Edward G. Robinson. From the movie "Night has a Thousand Eyes," 1948. Courtesy of Ron Stephenson.

Alan Ladd and Gail Russell from the movie "Salty O'Rourke," 1945. Courtesy of Ron Stephenson.

A scene from Gail's last film "Silent Call" with Roger Mobley, 1961. Author's collection.

Richard Lyon, Nona Griffith, and Gail.
From the movie "The Unseen," 1945.
Author's collection.

Gail and Allyn Joslyn. Sheriff Clem Otis questions Gilly Johnson
"Moonrise," 1948. Author's collection.

A scene from the movie "Moonrise," 1948.
Author's collection.

Gail fishing and not looking happy.
Author's collection

Glamour portrait of Gail. Personally autographed to Charlie's mother Mary Stella. Courtesy of Charlie Timmons.

A portrait of Gail portraying the tragic Angelique from the movie "Wake of the Red Witch," 1948. Author's collection.

Gail dressed in a shawl from the movie "Song of India," 1949. Author's collection.

Gail as Penelope. From the movie "Angel and the Badman," 1947. Courtesy of Ron Stephenson.

Gail enjoying her favorite pastime. Courtesy of Ron Stephenson.

Gail from her film debut, "Henry Aldrich gets Glamour," 1943. Author's collection.

Early shots of Gail. Courtesy of Ron Stephenson.

Gail looking frightened.
Courtesy of Tom Weaver.

From the movie "The Unseen," 1945.
Courtesy of Tom Weaver.

Photo by William "Bud" Fraker, 1949.

Gail at the time of her come back for "Seven Men from Now," 1956. Courtesy of Ron Stephenson.

Gail and Guy during a hunting trip.
Courtesy of Ron Stephenson.

Gail and Guy.

Gail and Guy with some of Gail's paintings. Aunt Suella kept the painting of the bull fighter in her home. Author's collection.

Chapter 7
Moonrise over Calcutta

Returning to Paramount after filming "Angel and the Badman" Gail should have gotten a much needed break. But Paramount didn't work that way; the studio rushed her into doing another film. It was this constant haste and pressure that Gail mentioned more than once as the source of her problems.

Although the experience of filming "Angel and the Badman" was a good one, her relationship with Wayne didn't turn out like she had hoped. Nevertheless, there were other men who were interested in Gail. She and Guy Madison were seeing each other on a fairly regular basis and she also spent evenings with Peter Lawford and Johnny Mitchell. Gail refused though to make a long-term commitment to Guy or anybody else. When asked if he had given up on her, Madison replied, "You were told wrong. She's a beautiful and loyal girl. Right now, were both very busy and we've made no definite plans but don't think Gail isn't on my mind, she is. And a mighty pleasant thought she is to have there too."[1]

Paramount's next role for Gail was a crime film, titled "Calcutta" that reunited her with Alan Ladd. Given the assignment of directing was John Farrow, husband of Maureen O'Sullivan who was known as Jane in the Tarzan films with Johnny Weissmuller. Together the Farrow's had seven children, with daughter Mia being the most recognized. Australian born Farrow started working at Paramount in 1942. Before he came to Paramount, he was a screenwriter and made his directorial debut working for Warner Brothers in 1937 on the film "Men in Exile."

With the outbreak of World War Two, John enlisted in the Canadian Navy. After his service, he returned to Hollywood and the director's chair, where he earned a reputation as a good director and an even better rake (playboy).

"Calcutta" is the capital of the Indian state of West Bengal. During World War Two, it was heavily bombed by the Japanese. With such an exciting backdrop, Paramount planned a film with lots of intrigue and dangerous adventure.

How much Gail knew about Farrow is hard to know, but she would find out a lot more in the days ahead. Working with Farrow on the movie was assistant director Herbert Coleman. Coleman began at Paramount as a script clerk before getting the chance to be assistant director on "Calcutta." He later worked on movies with Alfred Hitchcock; an experience he always treasured. The same couldn't be said about working with Farrow. Coleman quickly discovered Farrow was trying to get his former assistant, Joe Youngerman, back. But Joe was recently promoted and unavailable. Farrow then tried to get Cecil B. DeMille's assistant Eddie Sullivan, but had no luck there either. Left with no other choice, Farrow settled for Coleman.

"Calcutta" was the type of movie that Ladd's wife, who was also his agent, preferred for him. Ladd plays a bold pilot who, along with his friend Pedro flies cargo between Chungking and Calcutta. The female lead was to be a conniving femme fatale. Essaying the role would be Gail.

Coleman was astonished when informed that Gail would be taking the role and recalled his initial encounter with her. "The first time I ever saw Gail Russell was October 1942. We were filming the sequel for 'For Whom the Bell Tolls' on one of Paramount's stages. Only the whispered voice of Gary Cooper and Ingrid Bergman disturbed the silence that surrounded us. I heard someone move nearby. I looked around and saw Russell standing, almost hidden in the shadows under a light platform. She was staring transfixed with wonder at the beauty of the performance of two of Hollywood's finest artists. She must have sensed that I was looking at her, for she turned toward me and faded back into the darkness. At the end of the scene, she disappeared.

"A few days later one of the young contract actresses introduced us. The first thing I noticed about Gail were her beautiful blue eyes. But she was so young so shy. She seemed almost ready to run. Maybe she should have. There was a contract director, a handsome but immoral man from whom those girls that knew him shied away. He moved in and soon she was lost. I didn't see much of her between 1942 and 1946. She was busy with William Russell in the talent department. And singing and dancing with LeRoy Prinze, head of the dance department. I understand why she was cast when we met in Farrows office a few days later after I was assigned to the picture. Something had happened to her. The blue in her eyes seemed to have faded. She was no longer the eager, trusting school girl I'd met in 1942. I could see that she was completely dominated by Farrow. She was too anxious to please him."² Farrows own daughter Mia described her father as, "A womanizer of legendary proportions."³

Enjoying the trysts with actresses on the set was a fringe benefit of being a director. Coleman saw this first hand when one day he observed Farrow. "He'd disappear into his stage dressing room to be joined later by some of the young and beautiful would-be actresses."⁴ Gail kept company with Farrow after work, along with actress Beverly Thompson and friends. Together they'd go out to a joint called "Lucey's" and drink. Thompson remembered Gail would drink in moderation until Farrow would start analyzing her work. "Then she would have a few more Vodkas."⁵

Coleman didn't like Farrow on the set, "I didn't much like his style. He was cold, arrogant, and superior. He never seemed to know how he'd stage the action in a new set. He'd stroll in swinging his cane (his affection), hang it over his arm. (According to Barbara Eden, Farrow like to goose actresses with it, as Lanfield tried with Gail. Unfortunate no one taught him the lesson Gail did to Lanfield.) And walk around the empty set gazing through the camera finder trying to figure out what to do. He'd finally stop and tell the cameraman, the distinguished veteran Johnny Seitz, to put the camera there."⁶

Coleman, wasn't alone in his opinion of Farrow. Robert Mitchum worked with Farrow more than once and said, "He was a sadist."⁷ Gail's costar in "The Uninvited" Ray Millard described him saying, "He was the most disliked man on the lot, but a good director."⁸ Farrow's wife knew about her husband's affairs. She even had a private entrance installed to his own bedroom so she wasn't awakened when he came home late at night.

Coleman's first problem with Farrow while working on "Calcutta" was Farrow's insistence of, "real Indians from India working on the set."⁹ Coleman found the solution to this problem by hiring Indian sailors working at a nearby camp in Wilmington, California. Coleman felt that it gave the film a more authentic feel. As for the city of Calcutta, a little village street in Culver City was used along with a small dirt strip for the international airport of east India. The rest of the movie was shot at Paramount. Overall, the way it was shot the picture was not realistic and appeared low grade. Fortunately, star power helped raise the movie up to something that became worthwhile.

When completed "Calcutta" turned out to be better than expected and was one of Ladd's highest grossing films. The plot had Neal, (Ladd) and Pedro, (Bendix) ferrying cargo and passengers from Calcutta across the Himalayas. A flyer buddy of theirs is strangled on the streets of Calcutta. A nightclub singer informs Neal about her unsavory boss Lasser acting odd the night of the murder. Hoping to find the killer, Neal investigates, which leads to the fiancé of his late friend, Virginia, (Gail). Virginia feigns ignorance about the murder but Neal is suspicious. Over time, the two of them become attracted to each other. When Neal asks her about an expensive necklace she wears, he eventually finds out about a smuggling ring. When he confronts Virginia about the information, she pleads innocence's. This time Neal doesn't buy it and proceeds to strike Virginia several times. She then admits to being part of a smuggling operation and seducing the pilots who smuggle jewels on the planes. She then confesses to holding a gun on Neal's friend while Lasser strangled him.

A while later, Virginia catches Neal with his guard down and pulls a gun on him, but Neal wrestles the gun from her. Lasser shows up and a struggle ensues between the two men. During the fight, Neal shoots and kills Lasser. He then turns Virginia over to the authorities and reunites with the nightclub singer, before embarking on his next flight.

Out of all of Gail's movies, this is the one that most fans and critics agree she was miscast. Not convincing as a scheming deadly temptress, Gail was much better as a governess, teacher or a Quaker girl trying to reform a gunslinger. The problem was that there wasn't anything in Gail's character to bring out in this role. It simply wasn't there, no matter how hard she tried or how hard Farrow pushed her.

Paramount planned to put as many of their performers as they could into a light-hearted musical comedy film called "Variety Girl." You have to look really hard to spot Gail's brief cameo. She took the part as a way to keep busy between bigger roles. While waiting for a bigger role, Gail retreated into her little apartment, continuing her lifelong love of painting, and reading. She also spent time with Guy and the two became an item in gossip columns of the day. During this time, Gail spent some time visiting her parents and brother, who was busy with his band. Gail even went as far as to arrange a screen test for her brother, but nothing ever came of it.

Gail got a call to come to work a few weeks later. It was back to Republic for Gail in another loan out for the film, "Moonrise." The movie was based on a novel by author Theodore Strauss and penned in 1945. The novel had been serialized in *Cosmopolitan magazine* and published as a book in 1946. Two independent producers, Charles Haas and Marshall Grant purchased the rights and spent a large sum of money to promote the novel. Instead of a big budget picture as planned, the two producers made arrangements to film at Republic. There was no location shooting, and the film was shot on two sound stages to save money. The producers were fortunate, however, to hire Frank Borzage to direct, even though his fee came to $100,000. At this point, Gail was still drawing her lowly weekly pay.

Borzage, the son of Italian immigrants, was born in Salt Lake City, Utah in 1894. When he turned 18, he found work as an actor in Hollywood. Branching out from acting, he turned to directing and eventually went to work for Fox. While working for Fox, Borzage became the recipient of the first ever Academy award for directing in 1927. It was his fine work on the movie, "Seventh Heaven" that won him the award. He repeated this achievement again with the 1931 film, "Bad Girl."

The actor John Garfield was first choice for the lead role. But it fell through. "Because I couldn't see eye to eye with the producers,"[10] said John. Instead, an actor often called a B lister by the name of Dane Clark got the call. Raised in Brooklyn, Dane had done a little of everything. It was while being employed as a model that Dane first observed acting on Broadway and started auditioning for parts. His big break came when he was signed by Warner Brothers.

Dane would play the pivotal role of Danny Hawkins in "Moonrise" with Gail as Gilly Johnson. Ethel Barrymore (of the legendary acting family) was cast as Danny's grandmother. Allyn Joslyn plays the local sheriff, and Harry Morgan in an understated, but important role as the deaf mute Billy Scripture. Danny's friend Moose was portrayed by the talented actor Rex Ingram. Lloyd Bridges put in an early appearance in his movie career as the lifelong adversary of Danny. And even Borzage's brother got in the movie; being hired for a small role as a circus barker.

Borzage started the movie right away with ripples in a pond and music by prolific composer William Lava reverberating in the back ground. The next scene begins with heavy-handed music accompanying two pairs of legs walking in step to the rhythm as they ascend the gallows. Eerie shadows of the condemned and the executioner are the only glimpse of the deeds taking place. Next, a baby cries as the shadow of a toy figure dangles over his crib, suspended by twine encircling the toy's neck. The baby boy grows now leaving a schoolyard enduring the taunting of other children. One boy in particular enjoys tormenting the boy, whose name is Danny Hawkins. Danny's father was a criminal and was hanged; the boys in the school yard tease Danny never letting him forget it. All through school a boy named Jerry is Danny's primary abuser. Now an adult, Danny and Jerry have a final showdown at a dance over an exquisite teacher, Gilly Johnson. Stepping outside, the two begin to brawl and Danny looks beaten. Then an old flashback of earlier taunts by Jerry gives him a second wind. He flattens Jerry and emerges victorious over his longtime antagonist. Hating to admit defeat, Jerry picks up a rock and bashes Danny with it. In turn, Danny gains control of the rock. He then strikes Jerry, killing him. Panicking, he drags Jerrys body into the swamp. Along the way his pocket knife become ensnared on a branch.

Returning to the dance, Danny goes to the washroom to clean up. As he does so, he breaks up a bunch of people poking fun at Billy a deaf mute. As Danny cleans himself up, he realizes that his pocket knife is gone. If the pocket knife is found near Jerry, it could incriminate him. After leaving the washroom, Danny cuts in on Gilly's dance partner. The two dance and eventually decide to leave. While driving home in a thunderstorm, Danny has a flash back of the crime that causes him to lose control of the car and crash. Pulling Gilly from the wreckage, he pleads with her, asking if she is all right. Coming to, she reassures him that she is ok. The next day finds Gilly in a church singing a hymn with a group of people. A close up of her hands, the hands of an artist, shows her wringing a handkerchief, signaling the twisting emotions she is weathering in her life at the moment.

Danny meanwhile pays a visit to his aunt Jessie, the sister of his late father. Seeing he is troubled, aunt Jessie reassures him as best she can. Leaving her place, Danny waits for Gilly to come home. When she finally arrives, Danny confesses his love for her. Dismayed at first, she comes to the realization that she feels the same way about him. Gilly's chief concern is what to tell Jerry, but a close up of Danny's face shows that he knows the answer.

In the local pharmacy, the news spreading around town is the disappearance of Jerry. Danny shows up and orders a coffee. Hearing that there are plans to drag the pond where he dumped Jerry's body, Danny leaves in a hurry. Looking for his friend Mose, Danny heads to the train station. On the way he runs into Sheriff Clem Otis. Clem invited Danny to sit down and jaw for a spell. During their conversation, they notice the arrival of a stranger in town, getting off the train. Jerry's father greets his arrival and the two leave together. Continuing his conversation with the Sheriff, Danny becomes uneasy when Clem starts talking about Jerry and he quickly departs. Later that evening, Danny and Gilly meet and Gilly puzzles over Danny's uncertain moods. He questions her devotion to Jerry, but Gilly tells Danny that he is the only one she cares about.

Tramping through the backwoods, Danny arrives at the home of Mose. While the two engage in deep conversation, Mose offers Danny his philosophy of life and Danny admits fear that he might have inherited bad blood from his father. Mose does his best to assuage his friend's apprehension. Leaving, Danny takes refuge in a rundown mansion. A short time later, Gilly shows up and imitates a belle in distress, and the two then proceed to dance the night away.

Back in town, Danny spots Jerry's father with the stranger from the train station. The next day Danny, along with Mose and another friend named Billy go coon hunting. Treeing a coon, Danny climbs the tree to shake the animal off but while doing so he realizes that he is close to where he and Jerry fought. Gazing into the eyes of the trapped Raccoon, Danny senses a premonition of his own fate. Sitting around afterwards, the dogs pick up the scent of something in the pond. Running after them, Billy attempts to show Danny a pocket knife he found, it's the same pocket knife that Danny lost while dumping Jerry's body. But Danny is in a panic to find out what has the dogs aroused and doesn't pay attention to Billy. A minute later, the dogs discover Jerry's body. Agitated and frightened, Danny kicks one of the dogs in frustration.

The next day in the pharmacy, Danny examines pocket knives looking to replace his missing one. Sheriff Otis walks in, notices Danny and questions him about anyone having a motive to kill Jerry. During their conversation, Danny learns that the mysterious stranger in town is a bank examiner and that money is missing from the bank

Jerry's father works at. Danny knows that Jerry liked to gamble and owed debts. Following the sheriff's lead, Danny drops hints about the band leader at the dance the night of Jerry's disappearance and also denies being sweet on Gilly.

Later that evening, Danny and Gilly attend the local fair. They run into Billy, and Danny notices that Billy has his pocket knife. Danny starts to retrieve it but is distracted when he notices Sheriff Otis. Grabbing Gilly, the two buy tickets to ride the Farris wheel. During the ride, Danny explains the circumstances of his father's crime. He explains that the local doctor refused to come to his mother's aid when she was sick, which resulted in her death. In a rage, Danny's father stormed into town and shot the doctor. Telling his story to Gilly is a relief, until Danny notices that Otis is on the ride too. Unable to withstand the sheriff's gaze, Danny leaps off the ride to the ground, much to the alarm of Gilly. On the ground, Danny assures Gilly that he is unhurt as she hovers over him.

At Mose's the next day, Danny confesses to killing Jerry. He then hunts down Billy to obtain his pocket knife. In the process the two clash and Danny almost strangles him to death, but let's up just in time. Feeling remorseful, Danny leaves the knife with Billy and flees town. In the meantime, Gilly has been summoned by the sheriff to help locate Danny and bring him back. She finds Danny back at the deserted mansion, where he tells her what happened the night of Jerry's disappearance. Danny then asks Gilly, "What are you thinking?" Gilly expresses her fear saying, "Only how will it be tomorrow?" Gilly then pleads with Danny to turn himself in but Danny refuses. He then runs off to his grandmothers.

In hot pursuit with the help of Mose's dogs are the sheriff and a posse. Gilly refuses the sheriff's orders to go back and follows instead. At his grandmother's, Danny locates a rifle and is determined to make a final stand until he come upon his father's grave. Seeing it causes Danny to change his mind and Danny surrenders. Giving up peacefully, the sheriff lets Danny walk back to town with Gilly uncuffed. Gilly smiles as they walk into town and the movie ends. Her smile lights up the whole screen.

Did anyone give a bad performance in this movie? Gail as the sympathetic teacher remarked, "That's a funny role for me. Right now, I could hardly get through the first grade."

Working with director Borzage for the first time she muffed one of her lines. After the mess up, Gail turned to the director saying,

"Mr. Borzage I hope you are a very patient man."[11] Allyn Joslyn did a fine job playing the "nothing gets past him" sheriff. Harry Morgan (the deaf mute), without the benefit of spoken dialogue, conveyed his character brilliantly with nothing but mannerisms and facial expressions. Rex Ingram, a wise Solomon living in the backwoods, boasted that in "Moonrise" his role as a sage was, "The best role ever written for a Negro."[12]

One of the few criticisms of the movie was the part of Danny Hawkins. Most agreed that he was not very convincing as a southern country boy, especially since he and the other actors and actresses did not have southern accents. But then again, maybe it was a good thing, since too often accents come across as derisive.

Describing Gail's presence in the movie. "Her other worldly beauty was lit by an intense, melancholy stillness. With her long dark hair and white trench coat she looks like an angelic messenger of mercy."[13]

The movie unfortunately flopped when released. Republic was the studio where westerns were made and the film departed from what the movie crowd expected. Unlike Gail's other two films, "The Uninvited" and "The Unseen," which differentiated from their respective novels, "Moonrise" only slightly did.

Chapter 8
Night of the Red Witch

In an all too familiar pattern, after "Moonrise" was completed at Republic, Gail returned to Paramount to work another film. The film was based on the novel "Rear Window" and was the fourth movie Gail did that was taken from a book. The author was Cornell Woolrich, a popular crime mystery novelist of the day similar to Raymond Chandler who worked on "The Unseen." Woolrich gained such a reputation as a writer that he was sometimes referred to as the Edgar Allen Poe of the 20th century.

As soon as "Rear Window" came out, Paramount bought the movie rights and began adapting it into a film. The title of the movie would be: "Night Has a Thousand Eyes.

Edward G. Robinson had the lead role as John Triton. Robinson, a legendary actor, was one of the stars of the sound age. Originally from Romania, he and his family had immigrated to America as a way to avoid persecution of the Jews. "At Ellis Island I was born again," said Robinson.[1]

Taking up acting in college, he went to work on stages doing anything from errand boy to bit parts. In 1927 he appeared in a play about a gangster and it was a huge hit. As a result, the heads of several different studios made all kinds of offers to lure Robinson to Hollywood. He finally accepted a $50,000 dollar offer from Paramount for one picture. By 1930, Robinson had switched allegiances and signed with Warner Brothers. From there, he made the film "Little Caesar" and became a big star.

Robinson continued to make films for the next 12-years for Warner Brothers. In 1942 his contract expired and he choose not to renew it. Instead, he decided to freelance for a few years and in 1948 signed to do "Night Has a Thousand Eyes."

Gail plays Jean Courtland, essentially the co-star role. While Virginia Bruce and John Lund had secondary parts. The film reunited Gail with William Demarest, her co-star in "Salty O Rourke." Sadly, the film also reunited her with John Farrow, director of "Calcutta."

Robinson plays a carnival psychic who discovers he can predict the future for real and see tragic results. His partners in the act become wealthy because of Robinson abilities, so Robinson breaks up the act. Sometime later, his partners get married and have a child. The woman gives birth to a girl named Jean Courtland (Gail), but dies during the delivery. Years later, the girl grows up to be a wealthy heiress. The psychic foresees the tragic death of the heiress. Jean's fiancé, along with law enforcement, write the psychic off as a phony. But when they experience firsthand some of his predictions coming true, they waver.

A former business associate of her father arrives at the home of the heiress, and that night an attempt is made to kill her, but it's foiled. A second attempt is made, but the psychic intervenes and saves her. During the drama a trigger happy cop fatally shoots the psychic, ending his ability to see the future forever.

It was Robinson's acting ability that made the movie. He was a brilliant actor who could take even the most mediocre script and turn in a sterling performance. In the opening scenes, Gail and Lund appear to be hanging on every word that Robinson speaks. In fact, Gail seemed to be mesmerized by Robinson. Between scenes Robinson, a noted art lover, spent time talking with Gail about art.

Robinson's character, Triton, is a complexed man. He is torn between two worlds; the world he currently lives in and the one he envisions in the future. A tortured man with his ability to foretell the future, he looks to be set free from his burden. But only in death is this possible. Knowing this, Triton is unafraid and looks forward to being set free.

For her part, Gail was perfect as the doomed heroine that Triton saves. The real Gail Russell and her character Jean Courtland are identical; a sense of doom hangs over both. Gail's strength as an actress was playing these types of roles.

John Seitz, the cinematographer was first rate again. Outdoor locations were downtown Los Angeles at a place called Bunker Hill. The apartment of where Triton lived. The opening scene on the railroad yard can hold its own with the great opening scene of "Moonrise."

"Night Has a Thousand Eyes" is rated a good example of film noir at its best. Robinson however, never thought much of the film. It may have had something to do with director Farrow. This would be the only time the two would work together.

As mentioned earlier, several people didn't care for the man or his style of directing. Robinson wouldn't be the only one who found

Farrow loathsome. Tab Hunter worked with Farrow had this to say: "Farrow had years earlier made a showy conversion to Catholicism and was now a big mucky-muck in the Roman Catholic Church. But despite all his holier than thou piety, not to mention his marriage to actress Maureen O' Sullivan, he seemed like a garden variety lecher. I can't stand hypocrites and that's how Farrow came off. Plus, he was just creepy, with a pair of creepy eyes like a piss hole in snow."[2] Hunter worked with John Wayne on the film "The Sea Chase" which was directed by Farrow in 1955. Earlier Wayne made "Hondo" also directed by Farrow. After "The Sea Chase" was finished, Wayne soured on Farrow, commenting, "He took a great story and made a dime novel spy story."[3]

Unlike Farrow, Wayne would go out drinking with the boys in the crew, but Farrow believed in keeping his distance from the lower class as he saw it. Farrow had a lecherous quality, there was something seedy about him. During filming the movie "California," actress Barbara Stanwyck forced Farrow to apologize to an actor before she would return to the set.[4]

Lana Turner and Jane Russell both disliked making films under Farrows direction. On the set of "His Kind of Women" Jane remembered, "He was nice to us (Robert Mitchum) but he would be nasty to some of the other kids and crew. Needling all the time, if you needled him back, that was okay, but some didn't think you could do that ... other people were kind of terrified."

Farrow kept a bottle of rare scotch in his trailer that he would sample daily. A raiding party from the crew went into the trailer one evening and emptied out half of the bottle. They then ritualistically took turns peeing into the bottle. After that, Farrow would get evil grins from the crew every time he poured himself a belt of his prized whiskey.[5]

Lizabeth Scott, a contemporary of Gail Russell at Paramount, stated that Farrow was the only director she did not get along with. If Farrow had expected the usual affair with this leading lady, he was in for a bitter disappointment.

These stories and quotes about Farrow come from people who knew and worked with him. Finding a positive one is as rare as water in the desert. Some may counter that Farrow was a fine director. Just look at his work in "The Big Clock" and other movies. But one has to wonder how much of the credit really goes to the cinematography and the assistant director. Farrow did come up with a solution to one of Gail's problems. Since the start of her career, she had difficulty keeping her hands still. Finally in the film "Night Has a Thousand Eyes" Farrow tied Gail's hands together with handkerchiefs, which seemed to help.

Reviews for Gail were again varied. Brosley Crowther from the New York Times commented: "Unadulterated hokum. Edward G. Robinson plays the gent as a figure of tragic proportions, fatefully chained to a crystal ball. And Gail Russell plays the young lady whom he vainly forewarns against peril in a mood of melancholia."[6] The movie is more favorably looked on today.

Over at Republic, John Wayne was preparing to start his next film. Clearly missing Gail, he was going to ensure that she would be in the film called, "Wake of the Red Witch."

Contract player Catharine McLeod read the script and went to Wayne's office to see about a role in the movie. She found Wayne with his pals from the studio and he ignored her. "Not knowing what else to do, I gently laid the script on the desk and backed out the door. Clearly not getting the part."[7] Wayne, as in "Angel and the Badman" had casting approval and wanted Gail to be his leading lady; no one else.

John shared with Gail a special chemistry on and off screen. Harry Carey Jr. agreed saying, "It was most special with Gail. My mother said he definitely had a tremendous chemistry between them. Yet, I don't think it ever got into a big affair. He had a definite attraction to Gail, though."[8]

Knowing what Gail was going through at Paramount with Farrow and all the leeches, Wayne was anxious to hear from her. Republic agreed to Wayne's request, paying a hefty fee for her services. However, Gail never saw a dime and was only collecting her weekly salary.

"Wake of the Red Witch," meant a departure from the mystery murder film noir of Gail's earlier movies. It was also a change for Wayne, who had been making nothing but westerns for the last six years. Wayne's last non-western was "Reap the Wild Wind."

Based on the novel by Garland Roark "Wake of the Red Witch" was the first of Roark's work to be published. Taking place in the early 1860's in the East Indies, a sea captain by the name of Ralls skippers the ship, "Red Witch." The ship is owned by shipping magnate Sidneye head of Batjac.

Wayne portrays Ralls with Luther Adler as Sidneye. First mate to Ralls is Sam Rosen, played by Gig Young. Wayne's pal Paul Fix is ship-hand Arrezo. Adele Mara plays Sydneye's niece, Telelia. And Gail plays Angelique Desaix, the woman that Sidneye loves.

The film opens with Captain Ralls scuttling the Red Witch as it sinks along with its cargo of gold bullions. Subsequently, a board of inquiry charges Ralls, but under pressure from Sidneye, the charges are dropped. This frees Ralls to secure another ship with plans to recover the gold. Docking at a cove where Sidneye resides, first mate Rosen encounters the niece of Sidneye, the lovely Telelia. Invited to the home of Sidneye, he learns of the history behind the Red Witch and Ralls strange relationship with Sidneye. Clearly, Ralls is the kind of man Sidneye wishes to be—an adventurous scalawag.

Years ago, Ralls was saved from the sea after being cast adrift for shark bait; a fondness for native girls being his crime. The man who carried out Ralls planed execution was Commissioner Desaix.

Left to die, Ralls is rescued by Sidneye and the two return to the Island that Ralls was cast out of. On the Island, both Ralls and Sidneye are enraptured by the beautiful Angelique, (Gail) the niece of Desaix. Although she prefers Ralls, her uncle Desaix has already arranged a marriage between her and Sidneye. Angered, Ralls runs off in a furor attacking his crew and almost chocking Angelique.

Later, Ralls retrieves a sunken box of pearls in a nearby pool after killing the octopus that guards it. Celebrating his daring feat at a native feast, Ralls gets into a fight with Desaix and punches him into a fiery pit. Ralls leaves the island, only to return years later to persuade Angelique to drop Sidneye and run off with him. She refuses, so Ralls leaves. Later, he comes back when Angelique is deathly ill. As she dies, she pledges her eternal love for him.

Hearing this story, Rosen understands Ralls motives for sinking the Red Witch and trying to reclaim the gold: payback to Sidneye for costing Ralls the life of the only woman he loved.

Before Ralls can get the gold Sidneye has an aide blow up Rall's ship to scare him, but fears Ralls is dead after witnessing the explosion. Captain Muncy of the board of directors arrives to investigate the explosion, but Sidneye sends him on a wild goose chase. Sidneye and Ralls then make plans to retrieve the gold from the Red Witch.

While trying to get the gold, a terrible storm surrounds the ship that Ralls and Sidneye are on. The deep sea divers refuse to go after the gold because of the hazardous conditions. Ralls bargains with Sidneye about going after the gold. The Red Witch is teetering precariously on a precipice, ready to fall off any second.

Ralls descends into the depth of the ocean and gets aboard the Red Witch. He gains access to the hold and the gold but a load of cargo falls on him when the ship is violently tossed around by the sea. Trapped, the ship slides off the precipice breaking Ralls airline and plunging him to his death where he joins Angelique forever.

"Wake of the Red Witch" is comparable to "Wuthering Heights" another film about ill crossed lovers. Shot in 39 days with a budget of just over a million dollars, the movie did well and turned a profit for Republic. Gail, playing another doomed girl was fine as Angelique. Though in some of the scenes Gail's eyes appeared glassy and unfocused. There may have been a reason for this. Talking about working with Gail, Adele Mara said, "She was a loner, Gail was certainly a pretty girl, but she stuck to herself. I think the only person she ever talked to was Wayne, and probably because she had scenes with him. People in makeup and hairdressing would talk about her drinking. The rumor at Republic was that they had to take a lot of bottles out of her dressing room every day."[9]

Gig Young, who played Ralls first mate believed Gail was the best choice to play the tragic part of Angelique. "Gail was absolutely perfect for the part, because she has such a fragile quality. Well, she was fragile, very nervous and unsure of herself. I asked Paul Fix (Paul played Arrezo) if there was anything going on between Wayne and Gail and he said there wasn't."[10]

Of course, Wayne's buddy didn't know everything, no one does, but Wayne was no John Farrow.

Watching the scenes between John and Gail it's easy to see the warm affection between them. Sure, they were acting, but as the saying goes, the camera doesn't lie. Gail though was in a rut. "I've gone from jungle to swamp and now to another jungle. I think these are the same trees," she sighed.[11]

A humorous incident took place during filming of the death scene between Ralls and Angelique. Gail was lying in a bed with John Wayne by her side. As he began to speak his lines a fly buzzed into the Republic set between them. Every time Wayne attempted to speak his lines the fly interfered. A prop man tried using insect spray with little success. Wayne murmured, "If only I could get my hands on you." The fly returned again. This time Wayne tried to get it with the spray. Overcome with fumes Gail looked up from the bed sniffing and said, "If you spray this bed one more time, I won't have to act like I'm dying. I will die."[12]

Following the completion of the movie, Gail had a big decision to make. Would she marry Guy Madison?

Chapter 9
Hollywood's Dream Couple

"Wake of the Red Witch" would be the last time Gail did a picture with Wayne, which is a shame. She and Wayne could have teamed up in some of his later films equally as well as their previous movies. It's also too bad that the films that paired them weren't made in color. Films like "The Uninvited" and "Moonrise" are better in black and white because of the use of shadows and lighting. Republic later colorized the movies Gail and Wayne made, but it's not the same. Gail never was seen in her true glory with raven hair and sky blue eyes. And by the time she did make a real color film she wasn't the same woman.

During an interview, Wayne talked about Gail and gave advice to beginner actors saying, "If a kid came to ask me how to prepare for a screen career, I guess what I'd say would be to go to school, learn how to handle liquor, mix with people, get in trouble, work lots of different jobs and always remember your reactions to things and people. That's the best equipment in front of a camera. In other words, it's a matter of handling yourself. It's like sitting in a little room talking to somebody. If you react properly, the guy in the audience will go along with you. But if you hit a false note, he's going to figuratively get up and walk out.

"One of the best examples of that to me is Gail Russell. She had wonderful possibilities; her eyes are very expressive and very telling. But I think her home studio has let her down in not giving her proper grooming and teaching her to be at her best, that is, to handle herself. If it weren't for that handicap, I'm sure she would be one of our big stars. She was wonderful in "Wake of the Red Witch."[1]

Between her last movie with Wayne and her marriage to Guy Madison, Gail worked in several films, none of which could be called memorable, except for the fact that Gail was in them. First up was "Song of India," made by Columbia Pictures Corporation. Never known for their production values, it shows in the film. Gail plays a Maharaja Indian princess named Tara, who has just returned from school in America and is engaged to an animal trapper named Gopal. Together with an expedition, both travel into the forbidden jungle of Combi to pursue wild animals. Tara photographs and Gopal captures the animals intending to send them to a zoo. This raises the ire of Ramdar the rebel youth of a jungle village. The jungle where Gopal hunts is off-limits, but he remains undeterred. Native superstition rule that for every animal taken, a human life must take its place. But instead of killing, Ramdar frees the animals from their cages, drawing the wrath of Gopal. Ramdar then persuades Tara to go with him to Hawwar after valuable jewels. In reality he holds Tara hostage to keep Gopal at bay. As the movie progresses, Tara begins to sympathize with Ramdar, and starts to resent Gopal for his mercenary ways.

Gopal eventually catches up to Tara and Ramdar on a windy mountain top in the ruins of an ancient forgotten temple. At this point, Ramdar is attacked by a tiger that Gopal had wounded earlier. After the tiger attacks Ramdar, it runs off but returns when Gopal arrives. Ramdar and Gopal come to blows, and Ramdar disarms Gopal. The tiger then attacks Gopal, sending him off a cliff to his death. After the dramatic ordeal Tara and Ramdar realize how much they love each other. She returns back to Ramdar's village to live a new life.

With its higher production value, the film had the potential to be a very good adventure story. Instead, the movie plays like Bomba the jungle boy yarn with plenty of stock footage of animal filling in the gaps in the action sequences.

Gail may not have been too believable as the Maharaja's daughter, although she looked the part. In the role of Ramdar was Sabu, a film actor since 1937 of Indian origin. Sabu would become best known for his role in "The Thief of Bagdad." During World War Two Sabu joined the Air Force and flew bombing missions in the pacific. For his bravery and valor, Sabu was awarded the Distinguished Flying Cross.

Popular leading man of the 1940's Turhan Bey was Gopal the doomed fiancé of Tara. In a 2001 interview, Bey described Gail. "Gail was special, a beautiful performer. We had a good time making that picture."

The most noticeable aspect of Gail's performance in this movie is the complete lack of melancholy that marked her other films. Without it, Gail could be any actress before the camera, even upbeat at times. This change showed that she could play a part for whatever it called for. Although there were rumors that she had to be doubled for illness due to drinking, her close ups reveal none of the glassy eyes that were apparent in the film "Wake of the Red Witch."

It was a return to westerns for Gail in "El Paso" co-starring John Payne. This movie was the second color appearance for her. Not in spectacular Technicolor as "Lady in the Dark" had been, but in Cinecolor. Cinecolor was invented in 1932 by William Crespinel and had several advantages over Technicolor. Mostly this meant that Cinecolor cost less to process and didn't need special cameras to shoot film. The disadvantages were its color failed to compare with Technicolor. It did however, produce striking red, blue brown, and flesh tones. The majority of western films were shot in Cinecolor for this reason.

"El Paso" begins with former Civil War officer turned lawyer Clay Fletcher returning home in South Carolina. Wanting to see a former flame, Susan Jeffers, he makes plans to travel to El Paso where she resides with her judge father. Arriving in town, he discovers hoodlums have taken over due to the slackness of Susan's alcoholic father. He also discovers that sheriff La Farge is in cahoots with a crooked land owner named Bert Donner, who is controlling everything.

Clay is unable to convince Susan to leave her father and travel back to South Carolina with him. Things turn serious when La Farge and his gang attempt to run off an old army friend of Clay's and steal his land. Seeing his friend beaten by the sheriff for delinquent taxes causes Clay to stay in town. Later, he decides to represent his friend in court after his friend shoots one of the sheriff's deputies.

Clay makes plans to get Susan's father out of town to sober up for the trial. Now sober, Susan's father releases Clay's friend. This angers La Farge, who drags the judge through the streets killing him. He then rides out to where Clay's friend lives and murders him and his wife, but spares their son. Finding this out, Clay is hell-bent on revenge. Forming his own gang, he pursues La Farge and Donner. Susan becomes alarmed by the change in Clay and sends for his grandfather. Clay relents after killing a man, but when his grandfather is killed, he rides into El Paso. In a big shootout, La Farge is arrested and Donner is shot dead. Having restored law and order to El Paso, Clay and Susan can start over.

"El Paso" is no "Angel and the Badman" but on its own it is a fairly good western. As Clay, John Payne gives a credible performance in spite of the sometimes cliché ridden script. Gail, once again cast as a girl trying to save a man from himself, is wholesome and long suffering, especially in the scenes dealing with her alcoholic father.

Even in Cinecolor Gail is something to behold. Watching the film, a person gets a glimpse of the beauty that everyone spoke of. If only Paramount had spent the money on Technicolor to record it forever.

Another independent producer W.K. Frank was preparing a film about a legendary pace horse by the name of Dan Patch. The horse was a pure bred brown stallion born in 1896 at Oxford, Indiana. At birth his legs were so crooked he needed help just to stand. A local livery owner, John Wattles took the colt and with patience and care trained him. When the horse was fully grown, he was entered into harness races. Dan Patch never lost a race and huge crowds came to see the horse at fairs and races. By 1909, lameness had forced the horse into retirement. He passed away in 1916 and left behind records that took years to break. Known as "The Man of War" of harness racing, Dan Patch seemed like a good idea for a movie.

For the movie "The Great Dan Patch," Gail had a part that was right up her alley: working with horses. As tomboy Cissy (Gail) she helps her father run the livery where Dan Patch was born. The livery owner has a son that Cissy is stuck on, but he plans to marry a snobbish schoolteacher instead. After his father passes away, the son vows to make Dan Patch a winner. With the help of Cissy and her father, he turns Dan Patch into a champion, much to his wife's displeasure. Concluding that his wife is only interested in getting ahead socially, he finds himself falling for Cissy, who shares more of his interests. Together, they watch Dan Patch win race after race. It's another story book ending for Gail, as Cissy and the owner's son marry and have a child.

Gail's acting and appearance are about the same as in her previous films, although she looks rather thin in this movie. Playing a tomboy looking after horses was a good role for her and she grows in the part as her character Cissy does; from an unsure woman to a more confident one.

The last movie Gail made before her marriage to Guy Madison was "Captain China," which was released in 1950. She was paired with John Payne again in another Pine-Thomas production.

If Gail sensed that her days at Paramount were numbered with these productions, she gave no hint. And by then she may not have cared, because her contract was nearing its end.

"Captain China" is the story of a sea captain named Cinnough. Not unlike Captain Ralls from "Wake of the Red Witch" he is a hard man to figure out. Rescued after his ship is wrecked on a reef, Captain Cinnough, or China, as he is sometimes called, is seeking to clear up his reputation for losing the ship. His former first officer Brendenson testifies that he changed the ships course which resulted in the wreck. Brendenson is now captain of his own vessel and China books passage on it hoping to clear his name. While aboard, China gets into a violent fight with a former crewman from his old ship. Watching the two men brawl is Kim Mitchell (Gail), a passenger sailing to meet her fiancé. By befriending China, she learns about his past.

Later, a huge typhoon overtakes the ship, forcing Brendenson to seek China's help getting the ship safely to port. After China does this, Brendenson admits to lying in his testimony about the circumstances that caused the wreck of China's ship. As the movie progresses, Kim finds herself falling in love with China and leaves her fiancé at the dock.

Where both Gail and Wayne perish to be together in "Wake of the Red Witch" Gail and John Payne survive the sea to seek happiness.

One poignant line in the film is Captain China scolding a hung over shipmate telling him, "Peace doesn't come in a bottle, mister. I should know." Gail looks on knowingly as the words are spoken. John Payne, in later years commented that Gail was one of his favorite leading ladies.

Movie fans that liked a sea faring story were pleased. Those who didn't, weren't. Critics dismissed the movie altogether. "Hollywood should have left it in Iowa with the rest of the corn surplus. 'Captain China' is one of those screen voyages you fast forget. Gail Russell travels on the train with a full complement of the latest in tropical cruise fashion."[2]

It was in one of these dresses she wore in the movie that she got married in on July 31, 1949. The ceremony took place at the Baltimore Hotel in Santa Barbara. Maid of honor was Paramount secretary Mary Lou Van Ness. Howard Hill, a known archery instructor, was the best man for Guy. Other Hollywood people were there as well. Noted for their absence was Gail's parents and brother, which begs the question of why? This was the most important day in their daughter's life, and they were nowhere in sight. Did Gail want a small affair with few a people?

After the wedding, Gail and Guy headed off for their honeymoon to Yosemite National Park, North Island.[3]

Later in an interview Gail describes Guy as, "The one who understands me better than anyone else. It was my shyness that attracted my husband. Guy told me he enjoyed being with me because he didn't have to knock himself out to impress me. He said I was easy on the nerves. Most shy girls are, you know. An aggressive girl often has a tendency to make a man feel inferior; she creates a tense, competitive feeling. Shyness makes a girl appear feminine and helpless; this brings out the protectiveness in a man. It was Guy who showed me almost everyone is shy and has a little fear about making a good impression, but they're able to hide it better than I. When I told him I was afraid to enter a room full of people because I felt they were all staring at me he threw back his head and laughed. 'Honey, you're not that important. They're too busy wondering if they're making a good impression to give you that much attention.' That was the first time I realized that my extreme self-consciousness was a form of self-absorption and actually a selfish trait. I did my best to ease up."[4]

When asked about the moment she first started falling in love with Guy she said, "Who can say? I remember the first time I felt anything about Guy. It was after he hurt his shoulder falling out of a shower. He was in bed all bandaged and unhappy. Some friends of his took me along to visit him. He looked so miserable."[5]

Despite her love for Guy, they separated for a time after only six months of marriage. The reason however, probably had more to do with Gail; she was a deeply troubled woman with a severe drinking problem.

Chapter 10
Miss Garcia

Gail and Guy moved from their one room apartment and settled down in a rambling ranch home to begin married life. Guy would soon come to realize how distressed Gail was. The years in pressure filled Hollywood only made Gail's emotional problems much worse than they already were. To Guy's credit he stuck by Gail in the years to follow, no matter how difficult. Whenever Gail got in an argument with Guy, he escaped by going on an archery hunting trip with his pal Rory Calhoun. "When we quarrel," said Gail, "Guy usually goes hunting. Guy can always think better when he's away. I never fight back; I simply stop talking. Guy and I are different than most people here. We went into pictures so we could help our families."

During their courtship Guy learned to dance and Gail learned to shoot and ride. "My favorite exercise is archery, it has developed my shoulders, helped my posture, and made me stronger all over. I didn't know that archery was such a popular sport until I posed for some publicity still, with a bow and arrow, I got tons of mail from fans telling me that I held the bow upside down. So, I decided that if so, many people enjoyed the sport I would try it. If you don't get enough exercise, try archery. Walking to the target is good for you, even if at first you don't hit many bull's eyes."

Shooting at targets was one thing, a live animal is another. In several pictures taken on hunting trips with Guy, Gail can hardly hide her disgust while posing with a dead animal.

When Guy was away on a hunting trip, Gail resorted to her old habits of retreating to her room to paint. Guy always appreciated her "artistic touch" saying, "She has more talent in her little finger than I'll ever have."[1] While Guy was away, Gail was kept company by her pet Cocker Spaniel named Kelly.

However, after just six months Gail and Guy separated. Their split-up made great newspaper fodder for the gossip columns in Hollywood. "It's true," said Gail. "And that all I have say about it. If you want any further details, you'll have to ask Guy."[2] "I was moody. I'm practically over that self-indulgence and so Guy had to learn to just let me come out of my maddening rages of disposition.

I'd sulk. I'd flare up, or Guy would. Then we'd punish each other by staying away; silent and aloof. Now I realize a grownup looks absurd and withdrawn in majestic dignity. I no longer fancy it's fetching to be unpredictable."

Eventually, Gail and Guy reconciled and were once again a couple.

At this time Guy was co-starring in movies. After a promising start in the film "Since You Went Away," Guy's career had stalled. But it would soon pick back up. In 1951 Guy found his niche when he starred in the television series "The Adventures of Wild Bill Hickok," from 1951 to 1956.

Gail, on the other hand, was nearing the end of her contract with Paramount and had no plans to renew it. Nevertheless, Paramount had a movie for her called "The Lawless." It was another Pine-Thomas production. Not the last for Paramount, but the last for Gail. Joseph Losey directed this story about migrant workers fighting for injustice.

Losey, a native of Wisconsin, went to school with future director Nicholas Ray and studied in Germany after graduating from Harvard. Eventually, Losey made his way to New York, where he directed on stage, specializing in political drama. It was during this time that Losey learned the technique of making a visual point to audiences.

Arriving in Hollywood after World War Two, Losey began his career. But as a result of having joined the communist party in 1946 he was blacklisted. By the time of "The Lawless" Losey could only find work as an independent director. This would eventually lead to Losey returning to Europe where he would make the remainder of his films, mostly in the United Kingdom.

At Paramount, the best way to get rid of an actor or actress they no longer wanted was to put them in a movie that they knew wasn't going to be successful. This may have been what Paramount was planning by putting Gail in "The Lawless" and having her work with Losey. Years later, Losey spoke about working with Gail, saying, "Gail Russell, who didn't want to be an actress, was picked up by a talent scout when she was working at a department store in Beverly Hills and came from a lower middle-class family. (Actually, she had only applied at the department store.) She died of alcoholism because she was deathly frightened of acting, but she had the makings of a great star. I had a tragic time with her. I think she had the most beautiful eyes I ever seen. The most moving eyes. And she was immensely sensitive. She didn't know anything. Paramount had her under contract like a horse."[3]

Macdonald Carey, who played Larry Wilder in "The Lawless" stayed in the same hotel as Gail during filming. "During the filming," said Macdonald, "I had a room on the same floor as Gail and I remember the martinis coming up there before breakfast. I know because the first day a tray was delivered to me by mistake. She is a beautiful but tragic figure."[4]

Carey admitted that he and the crew along with a producer were drinking and dancing the night away at one of the local bars.

For Losey it was a chore to get the movie made with everyone drinking. "On the set I had absolute instructions from Paramount not to let her have a drink. The first time I shot with her I had a long night tracking shot. She couldn't remember a single line and it was three or four pages of important dialogue. And she grabbed me-her hands were icy cold, she was absolutely rigid-and she said 'Look, I can't act. I don't want to be an actress. I'm not an actress. I can't act. I never had a director who gave me a scene this long before. I can't do it.' And I said, oh yes you can, and you are an actress. 'No,' Gail replied. 'I've never kidded myself. I hate it, I'm frightened of it. Get me a drink and I'll be alright.' So, I said, you know I've been told not to get you a drink. She said, 'Get me a drink!' I got her a drink and she did the scene. This started her drinking and she was drunk throughout the rest of the picture. That isn't to say she was bad. I think she was very good often, but sometimes I had to disguise the fact that she was drunk."[5]

This conversation with her director only verifies what others say about Gail. She still didn't care for movie making and never would have been an actress if her mother Gladys's hadn't dragged her to Paramount seven-years ago.

Knowing that her contract at Paramount was going to expire soon must have been a relief for Gail, like a prisoner getting released from the pen.

Gail's last movie for Paramount is remembered today as a fine example of injustice at work. The movie deals with the plight of migrant workers in America and is as poignant now as it was then. The movie hit home with many migrant workers dealing with low pay, long hours, and terrible living conditions.

One migrant farm worker rose up during this time and spoke about these unfair practices, and organized the workers into a union. The man's name was Cesar Chaves. Chaves would go on to become a civil rights leader and fight for the rights of migrant workers for years to come.

"The Lawless" deals with migrant worker Paul Rodriguez (Lalo Rios) and his pal Lopo Chavez. The two pick fruit in Santa Marta, California. One day after getting paid the two head for town. Lopo runs a stop sign by mistake and hits another car. The other car is driven by Harry Pawlings. Harry and his passenger Joe Ferguson make a racial crack at Lopo and a fight breaks out that is broken up by the police. After getting a ticket, Lopo visits the Spanish weekly newspaper where Sunny Garcia (Gail) works. Lopo reminds Sunny about a dance that night. Later at the dance, Sunny encounters the new owner of the local town paper, Larry Wilder (Macdonald Carey). That evening a brawl breaks out between the same boys involved in the car accident. During the brawl, Paul hits an officer by mistake and flees into the night in an ice cream truck. Paul is eventually arrested, but on the way to the station the police cruiser overturns. Paul escapes serious injury and hides in an old barn. The daughter of the barn's owner is startled when she discovers the fugitive. In the process of running away, she knocks herself out when she runs into a wooden post. Exploited by others who see a chance to stir up racial animosity, she claims that Paul assaulted her.

Hot on Paul's trail are Larry and a dragnet, who track Paul to a stone quarry. There, Larry persuades the terrified youth to give himself up. In the meantime, Sunny befriends Paul's parents and raises doubts about the boy's guilt, but Larry is skeptical. However, he eventually concludes that Paul is innocent. Larry then publishes a story in Paul's favor, requesting funds to aid in his defense. The townspeople are enraged, and storm the newspaper's office, destroying everything in sight.

Larry, with the help of the local sheriff sprints Paul out of town. Returning to the ruins of his office, he finds Sunny unconscious. When she is revived, he's relieved that she isn't seriously hurt. Together, Larry and Sunny make plans to begin a newspaper at her father's business.

Paramount quietly released the film in 1950. It was seen first in England, where the reviews were positive. Macdonald Carey found the picture to his liking: "The Lawless" is a picture I can identify with. It is about a newspaper editor who comes to the defense of a Mexican boy's civil rights."[6]

After the film, Macdonald would go on to find great fame in television on "Days of our Lives."

As for Gail, her contract was nearly up at Paramount and they wouldn't see each other for quite some time.

Chapter 11
Lone Star

Gail owed Paramount one more picture before her contract expired, but she refused to co-star with Sterling Hayden in "Flaming Feather," so Paramount suspended her. With no plans to renew the contract with Gail, Paramount sent her to Universal International to appear in "Air Cadet." Their decision was more than likely a result of Gail's drinking. Reports of her drinking and on set difficulties were common.

Paramount was doing Gail no favors loaning her too Universal International. Known for their horror movies, they also specialized in low budget productions. The studio was kept afloat with the series "Francis the talking mule with Ma and Pa Kettle." Tony Curtis and Abbott and Costello were also big money makers for them.

Universal often barrowed stars from other studios because they couldn't afford their own. Loaned out from MGM, Ava Gardner had her breakthrough role in "The Killers," a film based on a short story by Hemingway. The movie planned for Gail would hardly be remembered in the same breath.

The movie is about a tough Air Force Major named Jack Page, played by Stephen McNally, who trains new cadets in Arizona. Undergoing all of the ups and downs of training, the cadets must prove they have the right stuff to be pilots. The youngest cadet falls for a woman named Janet (Gail), who is estranged from her husband, who happens to be Major Page. Seeing his wife with the young cadet, the Major is determined to have the cadet dropped from the program.

As the story progresses, the cadet learns his brother's death happened while under the Majors command. He blames the death on the Major pushing his brother too hard. Despite the animosity between the two men, they partake in a flight together. During the flight, the young man saves the Major when his oxygen hose disconnects, and he safely lands the jet. In the end, the Major reconciles with his wife, and the young cadet earns his wings.

Gail changed her hairstyle for this movie. Gone were the raven black tresses she had worn for years. Now she had a short hair style that the other actresses in Hollywood were adopting.

The looks that brought her to the studio's attention weren't the same either. Her face had taken on a more creased look. The years of heavy drinking and smoking were quickly catching up with her. In fact, her drinking was so bad that at times she would become seriously ill. In addition, she was underweight and ate very little while shooting. And as she did with previous movies, Gail would retreat to her hotel room and drink between shooting.

Despite her drinking problem, Gail gave an adequate performance in "Air Cadet," but it was clear that she was weary.

The film was shot on location at a jet pilot's school at William's field, Arizona. Included in the film were several contract Universal actors. Rock Hudson had a small part. Richard Long played the young cadet and Steve McNally was the tough Major. Also in the movie was a statuesque green-eyed actress named Peggie Castle, who in the future would share a similar fate to Gails.

Once back home, Gail took a much needed rest. Her movie days had come to an end. She could freelance if she so desired, but with the end of her contract, she hoped to resume her lost dream of a full time artist. Guy had jump started his career with the advent of the television. Taking advantage of the medium, he rode the range in "The Adventures of Wild Bill Hickok." Actors and actresses who were unable to find work in movies now had another recourse. It was the same for directors and writers as well.

At first, television was dismissed as a fad, but it would grow in leaps and bounds in the years to come. "When we went into production on the show in 1950, no one knew what the impact of television was going to be. The one thing it took was guts, because the studios wouldn't let their contract players appear on TV. We made a half hour show in two and a half days. That included dialogue, action, and everything." Reflected Guy. "We couldn't waste time on television."[1]

The success of "The Adventures of Wild Bill Hickok" set in motion other western series to follow such as: Cheyenne, Lawman, Wagon Train, Bonanza, and Laramie.

Guy quickly found that his TV show brought him back into the spot light and a little financial security. Collecting fees from merchandising and personal appearances was an added bonus. Guy was a good choice to play Wild Bill Hickok and character actor Andy Devine made a splendid sidekick as Jingles. Andy's son Dennis remembered how the show originated saying, "Dad's agent got a call from a producer nobody had heard of. His name was William Broidy. He had the rights to the name Wild Bill Hickok and wanted to make a television series of the same name. He also had an agreement with an extremely handsome contract player whose career was in the toilet by the name of Guy Madison."[2]

"Madison had run the gamut of pretty boy roles and he was such a wooden actor that bigger film roles would never come his way. However, in the '50s, TV was often a safe haven for marginal actors. In addition, Broidy got him cheap. He offered the second lead to Burl Ives, but Ives turned it down. He then offered the role to dad and dad excepted, but for more money than Madison."[3]

Dennis got to know Guy and Gail in the years that followed saying, "Guy Madison was pleasant, uncomplicated, and vulnerable. His lack of education or sophistication wasn't his real problem. It was his charisma; sadly, he didn't have any. Dennis sympathized with Guy saying, "Another big problem for Madison was his wife. He was married to Gail Russell, who was as beautiful a woman as you have ever seen. However, she was a chronic alcoholic, just like her mother. She was working a lot, and because she was so young the booze hadn't caught up with her looks. John Wayne took a special interest in Gail and had her co-star with him in two films. However, her drinking continued and Guy asked mom if she could help. So, mother brought her home and got her sober. Mom kept her busy and she stayed with us for over a week. Then she disappeared. Mom did this twice and then she gave up."[4]

This is the first mention of Gail's mother being an alcoholic. It could explain much of Gail's problems. Not all children of alcoholics become one, but they are at a higher risk. Children who grow up around alcoholics in the home develop similar personality traits. Adult children of alcoholics tend to bury their feelings, even positives ones like happiness and joy. Children of alcoholics tend to have low self-esteem. Their low self-esteem comes from others judgment of them, thus having the need to be perfectionists. Growing up around an alcoholic parent, children tend to adopt compulsive behaviors and are more comfortable living in chaos and drama.

The life of Gail Russell took another tumble when she was sought as a witness in John Wayne's divorce trial. If Gail was hoping to put her Hollywood past behind her and move on, she was sadly mistaken. Being subpoenaed to testify against the man she adored and, in a courtroom, full of strangers was more distressing than working on a studio sound stage. Wayne's wife Chata had never forgotten the time John had arrived home late after giving Gail a ride home (After the wrap party for "Angel and the Badman"). She now saw a chance to use this as a bargaining chip in seeking a divorce from Wayne. Much to his disgust.

"Why did she have to drag that poor kids name into this? I never had anything to do with Miss Russell except to make a couple of movies with her. True, we had a party at the end of the picture. Every studio and company does. Everybody was there from technician to star. I took Miss Russell home because she had no other way of getting home. Miss Russell's mother invited me in to have a drink. After a few drinks I took a cab. I came home at 2 a.m. and broke in the front door. Not because I was drunk but because I had no key and my wife refused to open the front door. I'm no saint but this is ridiculous."[5]

Gail, in a statement read by her attorney agreed with Wayne for the most part saying, "James Grant, writer and director and John Wayne, producer and director of the picture had surprised me by telling me they were presenting me with $500 dollars because they believed my salary had not been in keeping with the caliber of my work as a feminine lead. John took me home after the party. He apologized to my mother for his condition. He called a taxi. My brother helped him into the taxi and he left about 1 a.m. The next morning, he sent my mother a box of flowers with a note of apology for any inconvenience he might have caused her. I was contemplating marriage to Guy Madison at the time and was living with my family. It is upsetting to me that an act of impropriety had been placed upon the event of the day. I have instructed my attorney to demand a full and complete retraction under penalty of suit for defamation of character."[6]

Although it has been reported that Gail took the stand and testified, in reality the judge called a halt and granted a divorce to each side.

It was after this that Gail supposedly entered a Seattle Washington sanitarium for treatment. One paper reported the following: "Several days after the Wayne divorce action Guy drove Gail to Seattle for a stay at Pinel Sanitarium. But when they reached Seattle Gail backed down, refused to check in and returned home."[7]

"I couldn't force the issue," said Guy. "No treatment in the world does any good if you're fighting it. Gail has to make up her own mind." Knowing Gail's fear of strangers and unfamiliar surroundings, it seemed highly unlikely for her to undergo treatment in another state.

It was about a month later that Gail suffered her first public arrest on November 24, 1953. While driving at night, she pulled up behind a patrol car at a stop light and repeatedly honked at them. The two officers, Bert Dillinger (who know doubt took some kidding because he had the same last name as an infamous gangster) and his partner Ed Sweeney, got out of their patrol car to see if she needed some help. They found that Gail's speech was rambling and she was incoherent when they tried to question her. About all they could understand was that she was lost. After failing two sobriety tests, she was arrested and brought to jail. She was booked under the name Betty Gail Russell, age 29. Occupation entertainer.[8] Her bail was set at $250, which Guy posted to get her free.

Leaving the jail nearly hysterical in the glare of photographers, Gail quipped, "I haven't had my picture taken for some time."[9]

Later, during her sentencing her lawyer explained to the judge that Gail had been under great emotional stress because of her separation from Guy. In addition, having her name linked to Wayne's divorce also had her very upset. Gail was placed on two years' probation, fined $150, and ordered not to drink, avoid places that sell liquor and obtain medical treatment. After the sentencing, Gail fled from the courtroom, sobbing.

Why would anyone pull up behind a police car and lay on the horn? The police officers surmised she needed help, which wasn't the case. Gail had to know that she would be arrested. Was her action a deep seated cry for help? Was she releasing pent up anger or emotional pain? Gail blamed marital problems for her behavior that night. Guy had this to say about the situation. "I admit I'm heart sick over our separation but for various reasons we can't seem to make a go of it. I'm still devoted to Gail, anything she needs from me she'll always have it. She's over her illness. I don't think she will ever do another picture, though. She never liked acting or movie making in the first place."[10]

Guy had been more than patient with Gail, trying to make the best out of a bad situation. "My husband has been a tower of strength throughout my crises,"[11] Gail told reporters. However, at this point their marriage was doomed. Not long after Guy met model Sheila Connolly at a party. A few months later Guy filed for divorce, charging cruelty as the reason.

It had been a long difficult road for Guy, but he had come to a painful conclusion. The girl he loved couldn't be saved by him. "There were happy times at the beginning and don't think I'm laying all the blame on Gail. I know I'm not the easiest man in the world to live with. I thought I could make her happy, otherwise I never would have married her. Gail needed time to face things, decide what she wants to do with her life, Gail can do anything she really wants to do. Her basic qualities are fine and sound as anyone's I've ever met. It's up to Gail now."[12]

Chapter 12
The Comeback

The divorce of Gail and Guy took nobody in Hollywood by surprise. They had been living apart for several months and throughout their five-year marriage they had separated and reconciled constantly. But this time was for keeps. Guy was ready to start a new life and wished the best for Gail. The divorce settlement paid Gail $12,000 in cash, plus a yearly minimum of $2,000 to $6,000 in alimony based on Guy's salary. The divorce hearing took place in Santa Monica on October 6, 1954. Santa Monica had always held happy memories for Gail, but not on this occasion. Gail was too upset to attend the proceedings, so her lawyer handled everything.

A month later, after having been under the care of a physician for alcohol related hepatitis, Gail entered a hospital for treatment.

Gail entered the Good Samaritan Hospital in Los Angeles under the care of Dr. Howard Payne. This is the same hospital Robert Kennedy spent his last moment after being shot. The newspapers often referred to the hospital as a sanitarium, hence the confusion earlier that Gail spent time in a mental health sanitarium. Her confinement was sorely for physical reasons, although her mental state got a much needed rest as well. Finally, the hectic pace she'd been on since starring in the movies and marrying Guy was put on hold. But her condition was critical. The doctors described her condition as, "A very sick girl."[1]

There's no doubt that being at the hospital was a good thing for Gail. She was not able to get her hands on any alcohol and her liver had a chance to heal. It also gave her a chance to think about her life. "I think overwork and not having enough time to catch up with myself were the real causes," said Gail. "I always had a terrible feeling that there was no time. Everything happened too fast. I was in the hospital for five months. I needed a good rest, a long one. It was so lonely in the hospital in the oxygen tent with no one to talk to until I turned to the man upstairs, I had long talks with him. That's the reason I'm here today. When you're in need and scared then you seek someone bigger."[2]

Gail told reporters upon her release that she felt better than she had in a long time, she was ready to start a new chapter in her life.

Gail moved into a small apartment along with her dog in the Westwood area of Los Angles, close to the University of California.

Gail really wanted to get her life back on track. To do this she joined Alcoholics Anonymous, but even that wasn't enough to keep her from drinking. On February 5, 1955, Leonard Deutsch, along with his wife and daughter, were stopped at a red light. The next thing they knew a convertible struck their car from behind. The driver of the convertible sped off, but not before Mr. Deutsch got the license plate number. He contacted the police and told them that the driver was a pretty dark haired woman and that a black poodle was also in the car with her.[3]

If Gail had known that Mr. and Mrs. Deutsch's daughter Gail was named after her, she may not have driven off in such a hurry. Its possible Gail didn't notice the little girl in the car with her parents. Still, there's no excuse for leaving the scene of an accident.

The couple was reported to have been shaken up a little, even though the police reported that the damage was minor. Gail's agent, Yvonne West, told police that Gail would surrender later that day. This didn't stop the Deutschs from filing a damage suit of $30,000. The couple claimed they sustained neck injuries when hit from behind. Gail admitted liability, but contended that the amount was excessive. A year and a half later, a settlement was reached. Lawyers on both sides would only say that the settlement was, "For a satisfactory amount."[4]

In early July of 1955, Gail began wrestling with herself about making a movie comeback. A year previously she agreed to a movie saying, "I got up to the line but I just didn't make it."[5] Feeling stronger now, Gail contacted her agent to get her in touch with John Wayne. Wayne had promised Gail anytime she needed help to let him know. This could have been payment to Gail for enduring his divorce proceedings. Wayne knew better than most the emotional turmoil this lady endured, and had kept abreast of Gail's personal troubles by the newspaper. His company Batjac worked out a deal with Warner Brothers to make a film entitled "Seven Men from Now," directed by Budd Boetticher.

Budd believed Wayne had his own reasons for choosing Gail, saying, "I think he was fonder of Gail Russell than any of his leading ladies. And I think "The Duke" had a crush on her. She was my leading lady in 'Seven Men from Now.' In fact, he wanted her in the picture. I think she was the only leading lady that he really cared about in more than just a professional way."[6]

Burt Kennedy originally wrote the script for Wayne and Robert Mitchum came close to playing the lead. Wayne met with Budd and Kennedy inquiring who should play the hero. Recalling the meeting Budd said, "I think Wayne was sorry he didn't play the hero. I recall 'The Duke' came in to have coffee and asked us, 'Who do you think should play this fellow in the picture?' Out of respect for him we said, 'Duke, we want you to do it.' But for some reason he suggested Randolph Scott."[7] When asked by Budd who he wanted to play the lead Wayne casually replied, "Let's get Randolph Scott. He's through."[8]

Some believe Wayne chose Scott for reasons not all together noble. Duke and Randolph had worked together in two films in the 1940s but didn't get along. However, Wayne may have chosen Randolph because he was already committed to doing the movie "The Searchers."

Whatever Wayne's motive was, the movie turned Randolph's career around in a good way. Budd Boetticher and Randolph would go on to make five more films together, now considered classics of the western genre.

Shooting for "Seven Men from Now" began in the late months of 1955 at Lone Pine, California. Since the 1920s movies had been made there. The area boasts breathtaking scenery, rolling hills in the skyline and a beautiful desert floor. Its landscape was perfect for westerns. The Lone Pine Reservation is where the Paiute and Shoshone tribes reside. And movie companies sometime employed the local natives to work on a film.

Gail found the location to her liking. When she arrived in the little mountain town there were huge banners strung across the highway that read: "Gail Russell is back and we got her." Talking about the filming Gail had this to say: "It's been so long since I acted that it took a lot of grinding to get the rust out of the wheels. It's wonderful to be back at work."[9]

Being back on film location stirred up those old feelings of panic but Gail persevered. "Yes, I was very nervous in the first scene. All I could do was stand in a wagon and say, 'look' but I could hardly get it out. After that was over, I found things went easier."[10]

Budd Boetticher, a director that got the best out of people, remembered that her first scene brought up a crisis, and she drew him aside and said, "I can't go through with it." But some tough talk from Budd brought her around. "It was what she needed," said Budd. "Everyone has been kind to her. She needed a jolt."[11]

From then on Gail did better and really benefit from having a director like Budd.

The cast of the movie included Lee Marvin; a screen heavy that stood out in whatever movie he was in. Walter Reed was Gail's husband trying to make a go of it in the tough demanding west. Reed worked with Gail on "The Lawless" and "Captain China." (Reed witnessed Gail striking director Sidney Lanfield and didn't care for Lanfield either.) Reed felt differently about Budd Boetticher. "I'd say Budd was one of the finest directors that ever lived. All around he reads peoples personalities well. He knows who to yell at and who to be gentle with. I think he really was a psychologist."[12] Coming from Reed, who was a veteran of over 90 films and countless television shows that was quite a compliment.

Reed fondly recalled the actress in the role of his wife saying, "Gail Russell was absolutely gorgeous. She had the most beautiful eyes and was a terribly sensitive girl that you could hurt by saying boo! Gail lost her confidence on the film. She wouldn't do a scene. Budd took her back behind the wagon and talked to her. And whatever he said to her worked because she came back and did it, and did it well. She was a shy girl you had to handle with kid gloves because she was so sensitive. She had no confidence in her own abilities, which is amazing because she is such a great actress."[13]

Boetticher agreed with Reed adding, "She's not as pretty as she was before, but she's better looking. Her face has more character and she's bound to be a better actress, after all she's gone through. She had to fall out of a wagon smack into a mud puddle and she did it without hesitation; even came up laughing when she knew she was out of camera range."[14]

The director, along with Gail and Randolph Scott, rode to the location in Pine on horseback each day. Other cast and crew used vehicles.

Gail granted an interview while taking a break from filming to talk about her comeback. "They argued it was a good script and that I would be working with people that I knew, I decided to give it a try. I didn't know I had so many friends. It finally got through to me that I was letting them down. I was helped by having so many people pulling for me. I'd reach into my pocket and pull out a note from someone saying, 'we're praying for you.' I got a note from Jonesie Greenman (shrubbery expert) at Paramount. He has known me since I started in pictures and he never forgets an opening day. Naturally when things like that happen the tears start to come. All of them, from now on, I hope it will be one picture after another because there is nothing like work, physically and mentally. I quit acting to make a marriage and a home life, but well it was one of those things."

Gail also credited her long hospital stay with renewing her religious faith and giving her the strength to carry on. "I had always been close to God before, but my eyes had to be opened. Everyone has been very kind to me, but it's the man upstairs who pulled me through. We all have our problems, you have them, I have them, but I think I have solved mine. I hope so anyway. The past is the past. I'd like to forget about it and concentrate on my career. Now that I have my feet wet, I'm going to get them good and wet. I think the jinx is over."[15]

For years Gail wore a crucifix necklace, one you can spot by looking close in her movies. Her faith was to undergo many storms in her life. But no matter what, Gail never let go of it.

In the same interview Gail mentioned how pleased her parents were with her returning to film work. "The happiest about it is my dad. He has had three heart attacks and has been very unhappy. When I told him I was working again, he had to hand the phone to my mother because he was crying."[16] This is further proof how important it was to Gails parents that she be in the movies. Not only to her mother, who desired to be a movie star, but George so he could be known as the father of one. It also demonstrates the emotional traits of her father that Gail inherited. Both parents were pleased to see their daughter working again, not merely as a run of the mill commercial artist but a big screen film actress.

Although Boetticher expressed positives reviews to reporters visiting the set, years later he was more candid about working with Gail saying, "Gail was a complete alcoholic. About two thirds of the way through the picture she was going to play a love scene where she was hanging clothes and talking to Randolph Scott and she said, 'Budd I want to go back to the hotel. I'm not feeling very well.' And I knew she was going to go back and drink. I said, Gail, if you get in your car to head back to the hotel, I'm going to pull you out of the car and spank you in front of the whole crew. And she played the scene and she was great."[17]

"The night we got home from Lone Pine we had a big party at my house and she got drunk, and assistant director Andy McLaglen, who fell in love with her couldn't find her for three days. By the time he located Gail in her bathroom her stomach was so swollen that it looked like she swallowed a football."[18]

This is a tragic story that Boetticher tells, for it reveals that Gail had fallen off the wagon again, and her health was taking a beating from which it was going to be harder to recover from.

Budd was in a long line of directors who found it trying to work with Gail and getting a movie completed. That he did is testament to his capabilities both as a director and as a man. With Gail, he knew when to press and when to let up. The result became one of her best performances.

"Seven Men from Now" begins with the former sheriff of Silver Springs, Arizona, Ben Stride. Ben is on a man hunt, looking for the seven men who killed his wife in a Wells Fargo holdup. Stride kills two of the men early on. Back on the trail for the remaining five, he come across the ill-fated John Greer (Walter Reed) and his wife Annie (Gail). Assisting the couple getting their wagon out of a mud hole, Stride learns they are on their way to Flora Vista, California, where Stride believes the rest of the robbers are holed up.

At a relay station Stride runs into Masters (Lee Marvin) and his partner. Masters has heard of the crime at Silver Springs and plans to get the stolen money for himself. What Stride doesn't know is that Masters has been trailing him and the Greers. Annie cooks a meal for the group while Stride stands guard. During the meal, she learns from Masters about the holdup and murder of Stride's wife. She goes out to console Stride but gets rebuffed. However, Stride gradually unburdens his guilt of his wife's murder and Masters finally comes clean about wanting the money from the robbery.

On the journey the next day, the group, including Masters, set up camp. Both men are drawn to Annie, Masters for sheer lust and Stride to clean his soul. That night during a storm, Stride talks more about his late wife to a sympathetic Annie. And later, Masters makes a play for Annie with the results of being chased out of camp.

Masters arrives in Flora Vista and warns the Wells Fargo station robbers of Stride's approach. He then learns from the gang leader that Greer has the stolen money in a stronghold box inside his wagon. Masters then accepts a deal to help kill Stride for a share of the stolen loot.

Stride and the Greers part ways on the outskirt of Flora Vista. Stride then kills two members of the gang trying to ambush him, but is wounded in the fight and falls unconscious. Annie, along with her husband, locate Stride. Shortly thereafter, she learns about the stronghold box when her husband is reluctant to go to town for help. Stride tells the Greers to leave the box with him, knowing that the robbers will come after it. Annie's husband goes into town seeking the sheriff, but is gunned down by the gang leader after informing him that Stride is awaiting him in the canyon.

Masters then rides with the gang leader and his henchmen to confront Stride, but then double crosses the gang, killing the leader and his henchman. In a final dramatic showdown with Stride, Masters is outdrawn and killed.

Returning the stronghold box to town, Stride encounters Annie waiting for the stage. He tells her that he is heading back to Silver Spring, but if she ever needs him, he'll be there. As Stride rides away Annie has her luggage removed from the stage. She decides to stay and see what the future brings.

"Seven Men from Now" resulted in a great classic western in spite of some difficulties. "When Wayne watched it, he had wished he had done the part himself. He would have been magnificent in it,"[19] said Reed. Wayne's regret wasn't just that he didn't play in the movie, it was also that he missed another chance to work with Gail.

Lee Marvin made a career out of portraying evil characters. He had a rare presence and was able to steal a movie by playing the bad guy. "Seven Men from Now" was no exception, and Marvin was terrific. Gail's role of Annie was a replica of the conflicted tenderhearted woman that she had made her trademark.

Warner Brothers turned a nice profit. From their $700,000 budget, the film earned that much overseas and over a million in the U.S. It could have done even more according to Reed. "Duke was very hurt because Warner Brothers released it as the second end of a double feature behind some space movie. It was released badly. It was a very good film that somehow did not get featured billing."[20]

Reed ranked it as the best movie that he ever did. Others agreed.

Attending the premiere in New York, Ron Stephenson remembered how the audience went wild with applause when they saw Gail Russell's name on the opening credits. "People love to see someone make a comeback from adversity that has been written off."[21]

This movie was Gail's third in color and her last. One of the big disappointments of her career to fans is the fact she wasn't captured in glorious color in her prime. There were only glimpses in "Lady in the Dark" and "El Paso" which was filmed in Cinecolor.

In "Seven Men from Now" which was filmed in Warner Color, audiences couldn't believe this was the same actress from five-years-ago. Showing the ravages of alcoholism and heavy smoking, Gail had aged badly through her struggles with life and looked quite a bit older than her age of 32.

Chapter 13
Tattered Ambition

Gail returned to her little apartment after the movie was completed. Warner had already previewed the film to the press and received positive comments. Gail was cautious though: "I simply wish to wait until the picture is released to see if people really want me back again."[1]

Gail had very little cause to worry, said *Variety magazine*. "Gail Russell, off screen for some time, has not lost her appeal and is good."[2] However, most people remarked more about her appearance than acting. The face that got her discovered for movies was more weathered now, with a constant tortured expression.

Back home in her apartment Gail kept busy with her oil painting. She seldom grew tired of it explaining, "Painting has taught me to observe colors as I never have before. I love pink. I feel good in it. I feel awful in pea green and yellow is most unflattering. Colors deserve to be studied because they exert a greater influence than most people realize."[3]

Gail still kept in contact with Alcoholics Anonymous declaring, "AA is good for some. It depends on the particular thing that helps that person."[4] She remained determined in her battle with the bottle.

Bolstered by the good reviews of her latest movie, Gail accepted an offer from Universal to be in a movie titled, "The Tattered Dress." As with her previous films, Gail would be directed by a fine director in Jack Arnold, who helmed some of the best sci-fi movies of the 1950s, namely: "The Incredible Shrinking Man" and "The Creature from the Black Lagoon." Gail's new project included Jeff Chandler, Jeanne Crain, Jack Carson, and Elaine Stewart. This time Gail had a part different than her usual one. She would play a bit of a bad girl, something she never did in her other movies, except "Calcutta."

The movie starts in a small Nevada town where a big shot shoots a man fooling around with his wife. Later he is arrested by local sheriff, Nick Hoak (Jack Carson). A big city attorney, named James Blane (Jeff Chandler) arrives on the scene to defend the accused. During the trial (Gail is one of the jurors named Carol), Blane makes Hoak look foolish and inept, casting doubt on his client's guilt. As a result, Blane gains an acquittal, enraging sheriff Hoak, who vows revenge. Hoak then coerces Carol into making a bribery charges against Blane. Another trial then takes place with Gail as the key witness. A vigorous cross examination takes place with Gail refusing to budge from her story. But eventually she collapses under the strain, landing at the feet of the dismayed Blane. Hoak is so sure his vengeance is completed that he gives Carol the bump off when running into her outside the courtroom later. As a result, she becomes angry at Hoak and plots to retaliate.

Blane remains convinced that the jury will find him guilty, but with encouragement from his wife he returns to the courtroom.

Making a brilliant summation to the jury, he is found not guilty. Sheriff Hoak is tongue-tied and storms out of the courtroom.

Descending the steps outside of the courtroom, Hoak is overwhelmed by the crowds and media. Off to the side of the sidewalk stands Carol. Angered by his rejection and her personal reputation in a shambles, she pulls out a gun from her purse and shoots Hoak several times, killing him.

It was a pleasant surprise to watch Gail in an off-beat role for once. Those who dismiss her attempts at acting need to view her performance on the witness stand in "The Tattered Dress."

During the movie, there were a number of really good scenes. One fine performance by Gail is a scene where Hoak browbeats her into committing perjury against Blane. The rest of the cast did a great job as well. The rugged Jeff Chandler shines as the big city lawyer, Blane. Jack Carson, usually noted for his comedy roles, shows his versatility playing the unsavory sheriff Hoak. Jeanne Crain's part is small but noteworthy as the wife of Blain. And the sound track is by noted composer Henry Mancini. As a whole the move received positive reviews.

Things were looking good for Gail. Good reviews in her latest movies and making friends with singer Dorothy Shay had her feeling great. Shay was known as, "The Park Avenue Hillbilly" and recorded a few hit records for Columbia in the 1940s. Her persona on stage was dressing as an upper class socialite while talking like a county hick. Gail and Shay enjoyed a close friend ship. Some said it was more than a friendship. But the source of this information is in question. It's the same source that had Gail's birth name and birth date wrong.

At this time, Gail was still battling to overcome her problems with alcohol and was receiving moral and financial aid from Shay. In the summer of 1957, on July 4, Gail, following earlier tendencies, committed another drinking and driving offense, and it was the most notorious incident of her life. While driving a new white convertible, she veered diagonally across oncoming traffic, jumped the sidewalk, and crashed through the front plate glass window of Jan's restaurant. The wreck happened at 4 a.m. The only person inside Jan's was a porter cleaning up, one Robert Reynolds.[5] Jerry Reichman, a USC student passing by, aided Gail and the injured porter until the police arrived.

The injured ported was transported to Hollywood Receiving Hospital for injuries to his legs. "I've got great reflexes and I guess they saved my life," said Reynolds. Reichman, the USC student informed the officers Gail's car nearly hit his car before she smashed into the restaurant. A moment after the crash, he pulled the porter free from being pinned against a counter.

Hearing about the accident, Ron Stephenson drove down to have a look. "It was a sight to behold" he said, "with the windows broken, shattered glass and caved in front."[6]

Gail was jailed briefly then released on a $250 dollar bail. This disaster was Gail's biggest and the one she is remembered for today in Hollywood lore. She is fortunate that she didn't kill anyone or get herself killed. The porter escaped with a broken leg and several small cuts. Gail vainly tried to come up with a valid excuse why she was drinking and driving, as most do when caught. Her excuse was that she was on the way to visit her father who was ill from a series of heart attacks, the most recent just two days before. "I've been very upset about him,"[7] explained Gail.

On July 9, Gail was arraigned on a felony drunk driving, plus being sued for $75,000 by the injured porter. Her preliminary hearing was set for July 19. In court, Gail was very contrite, telling the presiding judge that she would, "Never take another drink."[8] Gail meant it but it was a pledge that she had broken before. The judge released her on $1,000 bail. Gail told newspapermen she was, "Very sorry it happened."[9]

Gail's earlier hearing continued to August 20, falling on a Tuesday. When she didn't show up a warrant was issued for her arrest. That night deputies were dispatched to Gail's home to serve the warrant. Sergeants Trail and Corbett were met at the door by

Gail's mother Gladys. Being told the purpose of the call, Gladys allowed the officers in and sought assistance. "Gail's on the bathroom floor. Will you please help me get her up?"[10] The deputies found Gail unconscious on the bathroom floor, barefoot wearing green pajamas with a half-finished glass of highball beside her. The deputies inquired if this was a suicide attempt. Gladys replied, "She drinks."[11]

Gail was transported to the prison ward of Los Angles General Hospital, where she was booked for failure to appear in court and placed under observation.

For the last ten-years of her life, Gail had been self-medicating with Alcohol. In the beginning, she used it to get through the movie making process. Alcohol took away her shyness, anxiety, and depression. Alcohol became Gail's best remedy for survival in Hollywood. It had now become her cure-all for dealing with any difficult occurrence in her life. Gail possessed the will power to stop, until faced with another crisis.

Her mother Gladys, also an alcoholic, saw an all too familiar pattern with her daughter. Using parental pressure Gladys forced Gail to undertake a movie career not of her choice. Gail gave up her true identity in becoming the movie actress her mother always hoped to be. Children, or in Gail's case, a teenager, take up a career to win their parents approval, respect and to make the parents proud (remember how Gail's parents favored her older brother George Jr.?). Instead of choosing the art career that she really wanted, Gail became the movie star Gladys wished for. When Gail succeeded in the movies, it was really Gladys. Growing up, Gail's second cousin, Charlie Timmons, heard all about how important Gail's career was to Gladys. Pushing Gail into becoming an actress, Gladys hoped it would open up opportunities for her too. It never did. Gail was able to obtain work for her uncle John Wesley Burton, a highly skilled blacksmith. He looked after the need of the horses used in film work.

Gail's attorney arranged for her release from the prison ward until her next court date to answer the original charges of drunk driving. Her attorney requested several continuances that dragged the case out until early 1958, when it was finally resolved.

Hollywood reporter Erskine Johnson paid Gail a visit in her small, neat apartment. Johnson described the place as, "On the wrong side of the tracks."[12] Johnson knew Gail when she first began acting 14-years earlier. She was 33 now with a trim figure, a mind that can think, the same demureness that made her famous on the screen and clear sparkling eyes.[13] Johnson noticed the walls of her apartment were covered with her own professional like paintings, Johnson also saw a frame with the printed words: "When God is going to do something wonderful, he begins with a difficulty. If it is going to be something very wonderful, he begins with an impossibility."[14] The same words, Gail informed Johnson, could be found on a mirror in her bathroom; the same bathroom where deputies found her unconscious back in August.

Gail took Johnson's hands in hers as she repeated, "Believe me I'm going to win this war." The hands trembled back in 1943 when Johnson first held them, and she said, "Hold my hands, I'm nervous, I'm scared." Now they were firm, steady hands.

Gail showed Johnson the stack of fan mail she received from well-wishers and how close friends like Dorothy Shay, Jane Russell and Roy and Dale Rodgers among others were pulling for her.

Despite everything, Gail endured in Hollywood. She told Johnson that she had no regrets. "If I could give advice to others who might get into the tangle I found myself in, I'd say get back to normality and nature. Space your time to take an occasional ride or a walk in the open. There is no medicine in the world as great as God and nature. I've got to learn to stand on my own two feet. I've learned you can be helped only so far. After that it's up to you. My only regret will be if I can't make something good come out of all this to give comfort to other people."[15]

Chapter 14
Cassandra

At the end of 1957 Gail said, "I wish I could just stay with my acting and forget the rest of my life."[1]

Gail would begin 1958 with a fresh start, but first she had to appear in court to settle the drunk driving charges of crashing her car into Jan's restaurant. On February 4, Judge Fildew found Gail guilty of driving while under the influence of liquor. She was charged with felony drunk driving but the judge reduced it to a misdemeanor. Commenting on the incident the judge said, "There is some testimony to indicate that the front tire blew out on Miss Russell's car that would cause her to lose control. But there is also evidence she had been drinking."[2]

Three months later, the same judge gave Gail a 30-day jail sentence, but reduced it to three-years' probation with a $420 dollar fine. The lawsuit filed by the janitor injured in the crash was settled out of court.

It was during this time that Gail completed a movie for Republic titled: "No Place to Land." The film dealt with the adventures of a pilot crop duster who gets involved with Gail. It is only noteworthy for being Gail's next to last movie. She does have some dramatic scenes dealing with an alcoholic husband that merit some attention, but the rest of the movie limps along.

Joyce King, the script supervisor for the movie recalled it was filmed in Holtville, California and was shot in thirteen days. She never forgot the blue eyed woman: "Gail Russell had been one of the most beautiful women in the world. But she had just come out of some kind of rehab."[3]

If Gail was recovering from some kind of crisis, she would soon be faced with a bigger one. Her caring father, the man who hunted his daughter down in Chicago movie theaters, passed away on July 3, 1958. Although not a surprise given her father's medical history, Gail was none the less stunned by the news. After a quiet ceremony he was laid to rest at Pierce Brothers Valhalla Memorial Park. His final resting place would hold a special significance for Gail and her mother in the future.

No matter how hard Gail tried to quit drinking, she never could give it up completely. It was the same with film work. Gail lived comfortably but modestly on the divorce alimony from her former husband Guy Madison. She didn't have to pursue job offers in Hollywood. But there was something about making films and drinking that Gail couldn't let go completely, no matter what. Both had been a major part of her life, bound together in some tragic pact with destiny.

Gail did no film work in 1959. In 1960, she received an offer that appeared to come out of nowhere to act in an episode of "The Rebel" starring Nick Adams.

Starting with the introduction of the "Hopalong Cassidy Show" in 1949, westerns were introduced to a new audience by the new medium of television. Guy Madison jumped aboard with his show and a new series as "Cheyenne." The show starred Clint Walker and helped increase a growing appetite for cowboy adventures. By the 1960 there were over 25 western shows on the home screen.

"The Rebel" series was the brainchild of Andrew J. Fenady and actor Nick Adams. A supporting actor in films, Adams long sought a starring role for a change.

Nicholas Adamschock was born on July 10, 1931 and was the son of a Pennsylvania coal miner.

From an early age, Nick was determined to seek a better life. When an uncle was killed in a mine accident, Nick and his family moved to New Jersey. Growing up, Nick was athletic and excelled at baseball. He eventually became good enough to receive an offer from the St. Louis Cardinals. But after reading what actors make for making movies Nick set his heart and goals on becoming a movie star. Hitchhiking to Los Angles, Nick, now 18, worked menial jobs while also working in plays, commercials and joining a theatre workshop.

In 1952, his dreams were interrupted when he was drafted by the Coast Guard. But after his service, he got a break when he was cast in the film: "Mister Roberts." The director, Mervyn LeRoy, became something of a mentor for the young Nick Adams. Other small parts followed, including a part in the movie "Rebel without a Cause." By 1958, Nick was working frequently in films and television.

Nick met Andrew J. Fenady after seeking the part of executed World War Two soldier Eddie Slovik. The movie wouldn't get made until 1974 with Martin Sheen as Slovik. Nick pleaded with Fenady to create a starring role in a series for him because he was tired of playing secondary roles. In four days, Fenady created Johnny Yuma, a former Confederate soldier roaming the west. As he does so, he keeps a journal of his adventures. The half-hour show premiered in October 1959 at 9 p.m. on the third-ranked ABC network.

Although Gail's offer to play in "The Rebel" seemed to appear out of nowhere, it was producer Andrew J. Fenady who conceived the idea to cast Gail in one of the episodes. Fenady had first watched Gail in the classic "The Uninvited" as a high school senior in Ohio. He was enraptured as others had been by her performance of the girl with the sad, breathtaking eyes.

Graduating from the University of Toledo, Fenady produced and acted in radio shows during his early career. Once he found his way to Hollywood, he started writing and producing television shows. With the success of "The Rebel" Fenady called the shots, keeping the show a hit. Even with his success he never forgot Gail. Watching the news or reading the newspaper, Fenady was familiar with Gail's sorrows. And even though Gail's agent was quoted as saying that, "No one would hire Gail for anything. Not movies or television," Fenady decided to offer the part of Cassandra to Gail in an episode called "Noblesse Oblige." (Noblesse Oblige is a French term for compassionate, honorable behavior that is considered to be the responsibility of persons of high rank or wealth.)

Fenady was a good example of this practice to Gail. However, Fenady informed Gail's agent that Gail would have to remain sober for the two-day $400 dollar deal.[4]

A few days later, Gail showed up to work at Paramount, where "The Rebel" was being shot. Walking through the gates brought back a flood of memories. By now, the first time she stepped through those gates must have seemed like a lifetime ago; unbeknownst to her, this would be the last time.

Upon her arrival, Gail walked into Fenady's office and remarked, "You know, Mr. Fenady, this used to be Charlie's office."

"Charlie, who?" asked Fenady.

"Charlie Brackett. He produced "The Uninvited." Replied Gail.[5]

As Gail quickly learned, Charlie was no longer there. However, other people Gail knew in the early days still were. Eddie Head, head of costuming, Nellie Manly, chief of hair dressing and Wally Westmore were still around.

Fenady asked Gail if she liked the script and she said she did. Gail then noticed a picture of John Wayne behind Fenady's desk.

"Do you know 'The Duke'?" she asked.

Fenady stood up imitating Wayne saying, "Sort of."

Gail eyed Fenady. "So, do I. I made a couple of films with him." She then looked at Fenady's stance and commented, "You know, that is just the way Duke stands, except with his right leg forward. More like this." Gail then took on the whole persona of Wayne; his furrowed brow and drooping shoulders.

"You know," said Gail, "the one word that defines 'The Duke' is 'honest.' He's an honest man. He can't be otherwise."[6]

Gail thanked Fenady for the part and left the office. The next morning shooting began on soundstage 17. Executive, grips, and electricians that had worked with Gail in the past came to wish her well.

The shooting got off to a rough start with Gail blowing the first couple of takes. She laughed uneasily as did everyone else. By the ninth take nobody was laughing anymore. Eventually, things got so bad that Fenady told the casting director to make some calls to get someone else.

After failed take number 29, Gail came up to Fenady pleading. "I'm sorry, really sorry. I know I can do it. Please just one more take."[7] Fenady instructed the director to shoot a different scene hoping to build Gail's confidence slowly.

During a lunch break, Fenady and Gail went across the street to Oblath's Café. Workers from Paramount spotted Gail and wished her the best. A waitress came over to Gail and Fenady and asked if they wanted a drink. Fenady blurted out, "No, No!" Gail looked at him smiling and said, "Please, go ahead. It won't bother me I've won the battle."[8]

During lunch Gail beseeched Fenady for another chance to complete the opening scene. "I know I can do it. Let's shoot it right after lunch."[9]

Gail was good to her word. She breezed through on the first take, never looking back after that and finishing the episode on time. When she was done, she kissed Fenady on the cheek and thanking him. For Fenady a wish had come true; being kissed by Stella from "The Uninvited." Gail then smiled and walked away. She had reason to be pleased. Many rank her acting in this episode among her best ever. Gail had recaptured her southern accent she used in "Moonrise" and underplayed her part brilliantly.

Moreover, the episode was good as well. It starts with the hero Johnny Yuma traveling to the town of Bannister, Mississippi to look up his former Gettysburg commander, Major Quincy Bannister. Along the way he is beaten and robbed of his pistol. After recovering, Yuma makes his way into town and meets Asa, the younger brother of Major Quincy. Asa has been nailing $1000 wanted posters for the capture of a man named Schofield for the murder of Mark Leversee. The town sheriff warns Asa to stop posting the posters, but Asa rebuffs him with a reminder of who put him in office.

Later, Yuma and Asa get into a scuffle with a couple of town rowdies. After the fight is over, Asa invites Yuma to come stay at the family home at Live Oaks Plantation. At the plantation, Yuma is reunited with his crippled ex-leader and meets their sister Cassandra (Gail).

While visiting, the Major laments that losing the war cost the social structure of important families such as his. Hearing her brother's spiel, Cassandra remarks dryly on upholding the family name, while placing a few rhododendrons in a vase.

A short time later, two bounty hunters arrive with a prisoner in tow: Schofield, the man on the wanted posters. Schofield declares his innocence of the murder he is accused of. Quincy offers the bounty hunters an extra $500 if they can get a confession from Schofield. Yuma warns Quincy against this to no avail and the bounty hunters depart for town with their prisoner.

Meanwhile, Asa is going through the belongings of Schofield when Yuma spots his stolen gun. Yuma tells the Bannisters that the man that held him up had a scar on his left hand. Yuma then decides to head to town to question Schofield.

Quincy, along with his brother Asa, head to town by a faster route to catch up with Schofield and the bounty hunters before Yuma does. Eventually, Yuma gets to town and finds the jail. He discovers Schofield beaten with mangled hands and a signed confession. Leaving the jail, Yuma recognizes one of the bounty hunters in a clothing store. He proceeds to question the man, which erupts into a violent fight. After the fight, Yuma makes his way back to Live Oaks and runs across a carriage in the woods. Investigating, he startles Cassandra and a man who runs off. She proceeds to explain to Yuma how the war damaged not only her brother Quincy, but herself as well. The terrible conflict of the war has reduced the ranks of socially eligible men for southern belles like her. Asa happens upon the two conversing and they head home together. Back at Live Oaks, Yuma still doesn't believe Schofield is guilty, much to the dismay of Quincy and Asa. He then learns that the murdered man Leversee rented a store from Quincy.

Yuma, with Quincy and Asa ride over to examine the personal effects that remain. As the trio starts to depart, Cassandra emerges from a side door where she was eavesdropping.

Yuma and the Bannisters arrive at Leversee's store. Yuma searches Leversee's living quarters and chances upon some love letters hidden in a vase. The letters are unsigned but pressed between one is a rhododendron, a trademark sign of Cassandra.

During his search, Yuma listens as Quincy reveal that the man Schofield is accused of killing was a former suitor of Cassandra. But Quincy considered the man beneath the social class of the Bannisters and blocked the marriage plans. When Leversee persisted and threatened to elope with Cassandra, Quincy killed him, setting up Schofield to take the blame.

With his evil plot exposed, Quincy pulls a Derringer on Yuma. Yuma draws his gun, but before he can fire, a shot rings out bringing Quincy down. It's quickly revealed that the shot came from Cassandra, who was exacting revenge on her brother for his wrongful deed. As Yuma takes the weapon from Cassandra, she proclaims, "The wrong man died at Gettysburg. All I ever wanted was somebody to love. I don't think that is asking too much." The line summed up Cassandra's disappointments and reflected Gail's life as well.

Feeling good after "The Rebel" Gail acted in the crime drama detective series "Manhunt" in an episode titled: "Matinee Monster." The episode was about a burglar who does his crime during the day instead of night.

While doing a job, the burglar is startled by Gail's arrival and strikes her as he flees. Interrogated by the detective, she gives a detailed description of the burglar. Later, along with other victims, Gail takes part in a police line-up, where she picks the wrong man. Questioned on her selection, Gail becomes indignant, leaving the office in a huff. Gail's performance in the episode is competent and she did a good job. However, she looked better in "The Rebel" without the pained expression and not as thin.

Before doing the episode, Gail tried to explain her troubles saying, "I'll have to use the word alcoholic because that's what I am. You don't get over alcoholism. You just don't drink. When I used to go into some offices, producers would ask me if I was drinking any more. They don't do that now and that's the best thing that could have happened to me. I guess there are still doubts about me. But you have to take the bitter with the better in this business. My moral is high. All you need is a little sunshine and a pat on the back now and then."[10]

1960 ended on a high note for Gail. 1961 would become as significant as the year 1924 in the Gail Russell story.

In 1961 Gail signed for a role in the movie "The Silent Call." Showing up for work, Gail was well aware of her reputation in the film industry. "Don't worry," she said to the director. "I'm well and truly cured."[11]

Distributed by Twentieth Century Fox, "The Silent Call" was a low budget film. Gail played the mother of Guy Brancato (Roger Mobley) Mobley was born January 16, 1949 in Evansville, Illinois and was the fourth of nine children. He began performing on television at the age of eight. Noticed by an agent, he was signed to work on the TV series "Fury" a western about a horse.

By 1961, Roger had appeared on eleven television shows and was 12-years-old at the time of "The Silent Call."

The film began with Guy Brancato moving from Elko, Nevada because his father has a new job offer in Los Angeles. Because there is not enough room in the family car, Guy has to leave his dog, Pete, with a neighbor. Unhappy, Pete breaks through a screen door and makes the long trek to join up with his owner. Along the way, Pete meets several people and endures some terrible weather. Eventually, Pete arrives home. Gail kneels down to him getting a bunch of dog licks in the process. Laughing, it's plain that Gail loves dogs. In fact, she trusted dogs and children, it was grown up people she was weary of.

Pete was originally rescued and trained by Rudd Weatherwax. Pete's most well-known part came in the classic, "Old Yeller."

The "Silent Call" ran only 63-minutes. Gail carried her part adequately; similar to June Lockhart in "Lassie."

"The Silent call" was the last time audiences got to see Gail on screen, and she didn't look well. She was thin and looked gaunt.

Roger Mobley fifty-years later had vivid memories of Gail and the movie saying, "It took less than two weeks to shoot. She couldn't have been paid much. She was only 36-years-old and looked twice her age. I ate some hot dogs during lunch, returned to shoot a big emotional scene, and threw up all over her. She walked me to her trailer and cleaned me up, a nice lady."[12]

No doubt it reminded Gail of the times when she couldn't hold her stomach down because of severe nervousness.

Gail felt that she won the battle with the bottle saying, "I dried out, I had a lot of time to think about the fears of my inadequacies. I reckon I've gotten to the top too fast. I was going to high school and the next thing I knew I was being groomed for a picture. There was this terrific mountain of work to catch up with myself. I guess the answer is I didn't know how to be temperate. I was so afraid people would think I was a bad sport. I realize what success did to me, it made me more than ever frightened of failure. That won't happen again. I've grown up. I'm stronger now. The future looks pretty good."[13]

With the picture finished, Gail retreated to her Bentley Avenue apartment.

Chapter 15
Not the End

The funeral service for Gail Russell was a small, private affair that took place at Westwood Village Chapel. She was then laid to rest in Pierce Brothers Valhalla Memorial Park, located in North Hollywood. The service took place on Tuesday, August 29, 1961. Dr. Leo C. Kline, a Methodist pastor, presided over the ceremony saying, "You know, as I know, Gail had a problem. You also know how desperately she tried to solve it. Beside Gail's mother and brother, people she knew and worked with at Paramount attended. James Lydon, who starred with Gail in her first movie was there and said, "Gail Russell was scared to death in that first picture. We had to walk her around the studio before her first shot. We had to stop her crying and being scared. She never got over her fear of film work and turned to alcohol to ease her nerves, it killed her at 36-years of age and three people in the business went to her funeral: me, Diana Lynn and one of her ex-husbands. So beautiful but so tragic."[1] (Other sources state that Guy Madison was not at the funeral, but did help with the expenses. Gail's second cousin, Charley Timmons was 16 at the time and attended the service with his mother and aunt Suella, but can't recall if Guy was there or not.)

Diana Lynn, a co-star, and lifelong friend of Gails was there and said, "Gail felt her life and career were going nowhere. She was drowning her sorrows these last three-years."[2]

Milton Lewis, talent head of Paramount was also present recalling, "A lovely girl who didn't belong in the movie industry. I believe she would have had a happy life had she become a commercial artist instead of a movie actress."[3]

Alan Ladd insisted on going despite his inebriated condition, and Robert Osborne, the classic movie host, was at the time a struggling actor. He sat behind Ladd during the service. Along with other mourners, he was shocked at Ladd's physical state: "He (Ladd) was devastated." Osborne remembered Ladd was fond of the lovely girl he worked with in two pictures.[4]

Gail's former drama coach, William Russell, paid his respects, but John Wayne didn't attend. Years later, he anguished over her sad fate: "God rest her soul. She died in 1961 after a long bout with alcoholism. I sure loved that girl but not in a romantic way. I know there were rumors, but I say screw them that like to think that way."[5]

Milton Lewis wasn't the only one feeling guilt ridden over Gail's death. Tabloid reporter Jim Henaghan, in attendance, felt great remorse over Gail's passing. He was one of the first to expose Gail's drinking in print, something Gail never forgot or forgave. "Tell him to go to the devil," replied Gail.

Henaghan knew Gail from the start of her movie career saying, "There was courage and honesty in the girl. But there was a fear she couldn't perform in the limelight. She needed help with life, she needed to like herself, to feel secure with herself, and then maybe she might have felt the world liked her and she could be secure as a human being." Furthermore, he said, "Movie studios aren't Sunday schools. They are not establishments of debauchery, but they are not Sunday schools. In the entertainment world there has always been certain freedom of language and deportment. The reason is that people involved in the expressive arts are generally less inhibited than then those in other pursuits. If one is a part of the uninhibited clan there is little trauma likely to result from exposure to a movie studio personal. But if a girl is shy and acutely conscious of the unfettered freedom on a movie lot, she can be easily shocked into a neurotic mistrust and confusion. This happened to Gail Russell. Now the girl with the eyes as blue as a wood hyacinth has slipped into eternal sleep."[6]

The last time anyone saw Gail alive is a mystery until now. Years after Gail's death, Ron Stephenson was casting people for film work. He interviewed a man named Victor who related an interesting tale. Victor once worked as a taxi cab driver in the fall of 1961 in the area of Brentwood. Late one night, he picked up a woman with her mother. After taking the mother home, the woman asked him to go to the nearest liquor store. She then asked to borrow twenty dollars, informing the driver she would pay him back when she got home. Once the woman got home, she invited the cab driver in so she could repay him. It was then that the driver noticed the pictures of movie stars displayed in the apartment. Inquiring, the driver discovered that his fare for the night was none other than Gail Russell. She offered him a drink, imploring him to stay and talk. But he declined, saying he had to turn the cab in soon. He then left. Victor regretted not staying for years afterwards.[7]

In the past, Gail had drank until she lost consciousness, but she had someone there to take care of her. In 1957, when deputies came to arrest Gail for failure to appear, Gail's mother happened to be there. This time there was no one present and the results were tragic.

It's terrible to know that this alluring woman came to such a dreadful end. But it should have never come to this. Gail's parents meant well, but there is a danger in pushing one's child into a career they that they have no interest in or may be beyond their capabilities. Gail proved she was a capable actress, but it took being reinforced with alcohol to do so. Not everyone is meant to be a movie star.

To pressure Gail into something that was not really for her would only insure she would struggle at it. As a result, the struggle was followed by feelings of shame, depression, low self-esteem, rebellion, frustration, and even suicidal thoughts. It's no wonder Gail wrecked her movie career. She didn't want it in the first place. You can put a large portion of the blame on her parents and some on the Hollywood studio. But Gail has to take some of the responsibility for her actions. Especially the times she chose to drink and drive, risking the lives of others. Several times she quit drinking and was ready to leave her film career behind. In fact, she went a time without making movies at all. But ultimately, she resumed doing both.

Gail wished to be remembered as an artist more than an actress. Since early childhood she turned her anxiety into creativity with painting. A shy, emotional child with low self-esteem, she grew up depressed and unable to interact with school mates. Art became her solace and helped her cope with life. It became a way to escape. Gail fit the stereotype of the frustrated artist who is in constant anguish because of her inability to change or achieve something. In Gail's case, she wanted to be successful and fulfilled in an art career. Gladys wanted Gail to fulfill her own frustrated dreams of being an actress. Frustrated artists feel alienated due to the perceived ignorance or neglect of others who do not understand or support them and the things they feel are important. They sometimes smoke, experience failed relationships and recurring heartbreak. In addition, they appear overwhelmed by their own emotions and inner turmoil, which is marked by being impulsive or adverse to happiness and fun. At times, Gail displayed traits of causing self-inflicting incidents. Frustrated artists like Gail are often self-destructive in behavior and are generally associated with mental health issues such as: substance abuse, personality disorders and depression.

Gail did leave behind her artistic legacy in movies. "The Uninvited," "Angel and the Badman," "Night has a Thousand Eyes," "Seven Men from Now," "The Unseen," and the underrated "The Lawless." Without Gail's presence in these movies, they would have been far less captivation.

Gail's mother Gladys passed away in 1974. She was laid to rest next to Gail and George Sr. Gail's brother George, a top record producer, lived until 2008.

Other key people in the story of Gail Russell including: Diana Lynn, Guy Madison, John Wayne, William Meiklejohn and William Russell are all gone as well. Diana Lynn, Gail's closest friend at Paramount, passed away tragically of a sudden stroke in 1971 at only 45-years-old. William Meiklejohn, the talent agent that picked up two school boys hitchhiking and learned of Gail Russell from them, passed away in 1981. William Russell, Gail's drama coach at Paramount, became an in demand television director with hundreds of credits. He worked until his death in 1968. Guy Madison retired after a lengthy career and passed away in 1996 after a long illness. Andy Devine summed up his former co-star in an interview one time saying, "The only trouble with Guy is that he never explodes. Not even when he was having all that business with Gail Russell. A man should explode every once in a while; he'd feel better for it."[8] Guy however, did not agree. "I did not have a bad time. Being married to a girl like Gail was a very great experience, a very great privilege."[9]

John Wayne in one of his last interviews before he passed away in 1979 mentioned that he watched one of his earlier films with amusement. He wasn't talking about the poverty row movies of the early days of his career. Duke said the movie was "Wake of the Red Witch." "The tangle with the octopus is always good for a laugh." But it was more probable that Wayne watched the movie to get one last glimpse of his wonderful co-star Gail Russell. Gail lived on in Wayne's heart, leaving behind an enduring remembrance of fragile loveliness to last forever.

The finale of the movie ends with Gail and "The Duke" sailing in to a new life accompanied by the words: "Wherever you go, whatever you do, I'll be beside you. This isn't the end, it's the beginning."

So, it is for Betty Gale Russell.

Afterword

After the manuscript for this book was finished, I was able to contact Bridget Madison, first born daughter of Guy Madison. Reluctant at first because of being burned in the past, she warmed up considerably when informed I grew up watching her father in "The Adventures of Wild Bill Hitchcock."

Bridget guards Guy's Legacy fiercely as any loving daughter would. Her father was a very private man who revealed little about himself and others, particularly Gail Russell, his first wife. Bridget was able to clear up some of the questions about Gail raised in the manuscript. Movie stars of the day were harassed and stalked by the media. This is why Gail and Guy's wedding was a small affair. Guy wanted to get in and out as fast as possible to avoid the media frenzy.

Bridget also said that Gail was an extremely nervous person and drank to relieve her anxiety. And it was due to her abuse of alcohol on her body that she was unable to have children. Guy stayed supportive and caring as long as he could, but it was an overwhelming struggle to help Gail.

At the time of Gail's passing, Guy and his second wife Shelia were living in Italy, where Guy was making movies. Bridget stated that Guy was not at Gail's funeral and had a strong dislike for them. But she said he may have helped with some of the funeral expenses.

Bridget never met Gail personally. She did gather from her father that Gail was a lovely girl, great artist and a good person. Otherwise, Guy wouldn't have married her.

"Maybe she never should have been an actress, she's so shy and sensitive that people make her nervous. She's a fine artist and paints quite well, but then no one is looking over her shoulder or watching her. She has such strength of mind that nobody can help her except herself."

Guy Madison

Gail Russell's Filmography

Henry Aldrich Gets Glamour, 1943
Lady in the Dark, 1944
The Uninvited, 1944
Our Hearts Were Young and Gay, 1944
Salty O'Rourke, 1945
The Unseen, 1945
Duffy's Tavern, 1945
Our Hearts Were Grown Up, 1946
The Bachelor's Daughter, 1946
Angel and the Badman, 1947
Calcutta, 1947
Variety Girl, 1947
Moonrise, 1948
Night Has A Thousand Eyes, 1948
Wake of the Red Witch, 1948
Song of India, 1949
El Paso, 1949
The Great Dan Patch, 1949
Captain China, 1950
The Lawless, 1950
Air Cadet, 1951
Studio 57, 1956
Seven Men from Now, 1956
The Tattered Dress, 1957
No Place to Land, 1958
The Rebel, 1960
The Silent Call, 1961

Bibliography

Artist to Artist, Clint Brown, 1998

Barefoot on Barbed Wire, Jimmy Starr, Scarecrow Press, 2002

Confidential: The making of a movie star, Tab Hunter, Algonquin books, 2006

City of the century: The epic of Chicago and the making of America, Donald L Miller, Simon & Schuster, 1997

Danger! Woman artists at work, Debra N. Mancoff, Merrell Publishers, 2012

Days of my life, MacDonald Carey, St. Martin press, 1991

Duke: Were glad we knew you, Herb Fagen, Citadel, 1996

Duke: The life and legend, Scott Eyman, Simon & Schuster, 2015

Fade to black: A book of movie obituaries, Paul Donnelly, Omnibus, 2010

Fallen Angels, Kirk Crivello, Berkley, 1990

Films famous, fanciful, frolicsome, & fantastic, John Reid, Lulu, 2006

Forties film talk, Doug McClelland, McFarland & Co., 1992

It's the picture that got small, Anthony Slide, Columbia University Press, 2014

Ladd: A Hollywood Tragedy, Beverly Linet, Berkley, 1980

Life and death of Thelma Todd, William Donati, McFarland & Co., 2012

Robert Mitchum: Baby I don't care, Lee Server, St. Martin's press, 2002

Stanwyck, Axel Madsen, Open Road Distribution, 2015

Science fiction and fantasy flashbacks, Tom Weaver, McFarland & Co., 2004

John Garfield: The illustrated career in films and stage, Patrick J. McGrath, McFarland & Co., 2006

John Wayne: The man behind the myth, Michael Munn, NAL, 2005

John Wayne: American Randy Roberts, Bison Books, 1997

Last of the cowboy heroes: The films of Randolph Scott, Robert Nott, McFarland & Co., 2005

Making movies black: Thomas Cripps, Oxford University, press, 1993

The Obstacle race: The fortunes of women painters and their work, German Greer, Farrar Straus & Giroux 1979

The Paramount Story, John Douglas Eames, Roundtable press, 1985

Shooting Star: Biography of John Wayne, Maurice Zolotow, Simon & Schuster, 1974

Tortured Artists, Christopher Zara, Adams Media, 2012

Your friend and mine: Andy Devine, Dennis Devine, Bear Manor Media, 2013

The Voices of women artists, Wendy Slatkinm Prentice Hall, 1992

Vincent Price: A daughter's biography, Victoria Price, open road distribution, 2014
What falls away, Mia Farrow, Bantam, 1997
Wild beyond belief, Brian Albright, McFarland & Co., 2008

Chapter notes

Chapter 1

1. Actress Gail Russell Dies, The Dispatch 8-28-61, pg.2
2. IBID
3. IBID
4. IBID
5. IBID
6. Untangle the knots within, Cynthia Anderson
7. Actress Gail Russell Dies, The Dispatch 8-28-61, pg.2
8. LA Times 8-28-61

    #Police report 8-28-61, County of Los Angeles report.

    # For most her life Gail kept a dog of some kind, which may have alerted her neighbors. There is no record if one was present.

Chapter 2

1. Kirk Crivello, Fallen Angels, 1998, pg.21
2. Reading Eagle, 11-25-53, pg.2
3. Ancestry.com
4. Birth certificate, Cook County
5. Ancestry.com
6. IBID
7. Kirk Crivello, Fallen Angels, 1998, pg20
8. Classic Images, No.268 pg.24
9. Kirk Crivello, Fallen Angels, 1998, pg.20
10. Tom Weaver, Science Fiction and Fantasy Film Flashbacks, 2001, pg.18
11. Photoplay, March, 1954, Guy Madison's heartbreak marriage, pg.90
12. Kirk Crivello, Fallen Angels, 1998, pg20

13. Motion picture magazine, November 1950 Helen Weller, Confessions of an introvert, pg.38
14. St. Petersburg Times, 11-9-44, pg.15

    #one of the general rule for filling out a birth certificate is to verify with the mother the spelling of the names, especially those that have different spellings for the same sound, such as Emily or Emilee, Joh or John Gail or Gale. The registrar simply may have spelled it their way. Gail being the correct way in the first place.

    #Animals can ease social anxiety in children, Gail liked pets as companions instead of her peers.

    #The Russells in 1930 employed a servant, Edna Williams. Other census reports list Elizabeth L. "Gail" Russell as niece staying with relatives. This is where the confusion probably started over Gail's name. In line with Gail being shipped out to her uncle's farm in Michigan, it makes you wonder if Gail was the odd kid out or simply the Russell were experiencing difficulties.

    # Maternal over control, parent child interactions, abandonment, rejection, sexual abuse, a family conflict, or some other negative experience is related to child social anxiety and depression. Genetic factors have been implicated as well.

    # No relation to Charles Russell, well known western painter.

Chapter 3
1. Kirk Crivello, Fallen Angels, 1998, pg.20
2. Michael Munn: John Wayne the man behind the myth, 2003 pg.157
3. Kirk Crivello, Fallen Angels, 1998, pg.20
4. IBID
5. Motion picture magazine, November, 1950 Helen Weller, Confession of an introvert, pg.38
6. Interview with school administrator, 7-5-14

7. The Milwaukee journal, 5-15-44, pg.33
8. IBID
9. Anthony Slide, It's the pictures that got small, 2014 pg.214
10. Louella Parsons, St. Petersburg Times: Gail Russell found fame, 2-18-45, pg.65
11. Kirk Crivello, Fallen Angels, 1998, pg.21
12. LA Times 6-7-2007
13. Kirk Crivello, Fallen Angels, 1998, pg.21
14. IBID
15. Sister Celluloid 9-21-14
16. Ladd: A Hollywood tragedy, Beverly Linet, 1979, pg.53
17. The daily reporter, Hollywood today, Erskine Johnson, pg.1

#Charlie Bates or Cates wrote Gail a fan letter from overseas while serving in WW2. She invited him out to Hollywood for a studio tour. Although it was reported that Gail was overjoyed to hear from one of the boys who brought her to the attention of Meiklejohn, knowing how she really felt about being discovered this doesn't seem likely.

Gail later transferred to University High School when the Russells moved back to Santa Monica. Some sources list her as going to Santa Monica High. As with her name and correct birth date I sought to clear up exactly where she went to high school. I contacted Santa Monica High School first, but drew a blank. However, when I called University High, I had better success. The school still had Gail Russell's school record. She enrolled on September 1940, and left the school in February 1942. The records also indicated that she was going to Santa Monica Tech

Chapter 4

1. Lewiston evening journal, 4-28-45, pg.9

2. The Milwaukee journal, All in a day's work for a talent finder., Sue Chamber, 3-18-45, pg.19
3. Films of the Golden Age, Magazine No. 77, Uninvited consequences, Tom Weaver
4. Kirk Crivello, Fallen Angels, 1998, pg.21
5. Motion picture magazine, November, 1950, Helen Weller, Confessions of an introvert, pg.38
6. IBID
7. Pittsburg post-gazette, Starlet gets rough treatment, 3-22-43, pg.57
8. Kirk Crivello, Fallen Angels, 1998, pg.21
9. IBID
10. IBID
11. Anthony Slide, It's the picture that got small, 2014, pg.210
12. Tom Weaver, Science fiction and fantasy flashbacks, 2001, pg17
13. Anthony Slide, It's the picture that got small, 2014, pg.210
14. IBID
15. Tom Weaver, Science fiction and fantasy flashbacks, 2001, pg18
16. Tom Weaver; It came from Hollywood, 2004 pg.241
17. Anthony Slide, It's the picture that got small, 2014, pg.216
18. Scarlet street magazine, issue 12, fall 1993, pg.28
19. Anthony Slide, It's the picture that got small, 2014, pg.216
20. IBID
21. IBID
22. Tom Weaver, Science fiction and fantasy flashbacks, 2001, pg.28
23. Scarlet street magazine, issue 12, fall 1993, pg.28
24. Tom Weaver, Science fiction and fantasy flashbacks, 2001, pg.18
25. Anthony Slide, It's the picture that got small, 2014, pg.220
26. IBID
27. IBID
28. IBID

29. Scarlet street magazine, issue 12, fall 1993, pg.28
30. Maximillian De Lafayette, Hollywood's most beautiful exclusive and rarest photo album, 2010, pg.72

#Very disappointed in not getting the role of Stella, June Lockhart in an interview claimed the casting director as Paramount personally brought Gail in to get the part.

After Gail passing Charlie's mother Mary Stella, Grandmother Ruth Emma and Aunt Suella were left several of Gails personal effects: The longbow, riding crop, painting table, paintings, and an autographed picture.

Chapter 5

1. Scarlet street magazine, issue 12, fall 1993, pg.28
2. IBID
3. Doug McClelland, Forties film talk, 1992, pg.235
4. The Palm Beach post, 11-15-44, Young film star Gail Russell recalls early career struggles, pg.3
5. Tom Weaver, Science fiction and fantasy flashbacks, 2001, pg.18
6. Anthony Slide, It's the picture that got small, 2014, pg.226
7. Doug McClelland, Forties film talk, 1992, pg.235
8. Tom Weaver, Science fiction and fantasy flashbacks, 2001, pg.22
9. Glamour girl of the silver screen
10. IBID
11. The Coaticook Observer, 4-20-45, pg.4 Gail Russell wears Cinderella Slippers.
12. Kirk Crivello, Fallen Angels, 1998, pg.21
13. Bobbin Coons, Hollywood Sights and sounds, pg.3
14. The evening independent, theatre gossip, 2-23-45, pg.15
15. The Sherbrook telegram, Hollywood round up, 4-27-45, pg.8

16. The Coaticook observer, Gail Russell learns from famous lovers, 5-25-45
17. Tom Weaver, Science fiction and fantasy flashbacks, 2001, pg.22
18. IBID
19. The Montreal Gazette, The unseen first rate thriller, 4-28-45, pg.21
20. The Milwaukee journal, Gail goes along nicely, 6-10-45, pg.27
21. Tom Weaver: I am a monster movie maker, 2001, pg.153
22. Kirk Crivello, fallen angels, 1988, pg.22
23. Palm Beach daily news, Louella Parsons says, 2-13-45, pg.37
24. Doug McClelland, Forties film talk, 1992, pg.235
25. Conversation with Ron Stephenson
26. IBID

#Gail received her first souvenir from a G.I. infantrymen admirers overseas. Gail was sent a piece of glass from a Herman plane shot down over Italy. The boys explained they had seen an outdoor showing of "The Uninvited" and since they were as scared as she was in the movie, she should have the souvenir. (Pittsburg press, 12-26-44).

#According to Ray Milland, Marshall pursued Gail during the making of "The Unseen."

Source: Ron Stephenson, Photography magazine, March, 1956 makes the same claim. It says that Gail underwent a similar experience in "The Uninvited" with a cast member,

#Gail made a brief appearance in Duffy's Tavern serenade by Bing Crosby along with other starlets.

Chapter 6

1. Maurice Zolotow: Shooting Star, A biography of John Wayne, pg. 197
2. Herb Fagen: Duke we're glad we knew you, 1996, pg.66
3. Herald Journal, Gail Russell encounters cattle, cactus, and sand, 6-30-46, pg.66

4. Michael Munn, John Wayne the man behind the myth, 2003, pg. 57
5. Scarlet Street Magazine, No.15, summer 1994, pg.75
6. Ultra Filmfax Magazine, No.63-64, pg.75
7. Scarlet Street Magazine, No.29, pg.43
8. William Donati: The life and death of Thelma Todd, 2012, pg.1
9. Randy Roberts, John Wayne: America, 1997, pg.283
10. IBID
11. IBID
12. IBID
13. IBID
14. Daytona Beach Morning Journal, 5-16-1947, pg.45

\# Other sources have just about everyone at the studio getting involved with Gail, but this is the young lady who struck a director for getting out of line.

\# Gail revealed to Charlie's father Joe that John Wayne suffered from the worst breath she ever encountered, which makes you sympathize with Gail in her kissing scene with him. Source Charlie Timmons.

\# Website for Cottonwood Hotel interviewed a couple of women who were little girls at the time of the shooting for "Angel and the Badman." Both recall John Wayne staying there and his close relationship with his co-star. # Shirley Temple, Larry King interview.

Chapter 7

1. St. Petersburg Times, Guy Madison, "I keep my eyes open and my big mouth shut." 7-7-46. pg.66
2. Herbert Coleman, The man who knew Hitchcock, 2007, pg.125
3. Mia Farrow, What falls away, 1996, pg.148
4. Herbert Coleman, The man who knew Hitchcock, 2007, pg.126
5. Kirk Crivello, Fallen Angles, 1998, pg.28
6. Herbert Coleman, The man who knew Hitchcock, 2007, pg.127

7. Lee Sever, Robert Mitchum: Baby I just don't care, 2002
8. John Reed, Films famous, fanciful, frolicsome & fantastic, 2006, pg.4
9. Herbert Coleman, The man who knew Hitchcock, 2007, pg.127
10. Patrick J. McGrath, John Garfield: The illustrated career in films and stage, 1993, pg.114
11. Toledo Blade, All forgiven, John Todd, 1-6-48
12. Thomas Cripps University, Making movies black, 1993, pg.207
13. Imogen Sara Smith, In lonely places: Film noir beyond the city, 2011, pg.99

Chapter 8
1. Barry Moreno, Ellis Island, 2008, pg.99
2. Tab Hunter, Confidential: The making of a movie star, 2006, pg.104
3. Scott Eyman, John Wayne: The life and legend, 2015, pg.262
4. Axel Madsen, Stanwyck, 2001, pg.238
5. Lee Sever, Robert Mitchum: Baby I don't care, 2002, pg.210
6. N.Y Times, 10-14-48
7. Ronald L. Davis, Duke: The life and times of John Wayne, 2012, pg.137
8. Herb Fagen, Duke, were glad we knew you, 1996, pg.67
9. Ronald L. Davis, Duke: The life and times of John Wayne, 2012, pg.67
10. IBID
11. The Evening Independent, 7-31-48
12. St. Petersburg Times, 9-12-48, pg.49

Chapter 9
1. Hedda Hopper, The Miami News, Wayne 22-years in film, "retire unknown word." 2-12-49, pg.45
2. Leo Miller, Sunday Herald, Is the trip necessary, 6-11-50, pg.15

3. Eugene Register Guard, Gail Russell weds actor Guy Madison, 8-7-49, pg.58
4. Motion Picture magazine, November 1950, Hellen Weller, Confessions of an introvert, pg.64-65
5. Modern screen magazine, April, 1950, They don't belong, pg.43
    # Bridget Madison is adamant the rumors about her father were just that, rumors and unfounded. Guy even joked about it. The rumors began because of Henry Willson Guy's agent.

Chapter 10
1. Photoplay, March, 1954, Guy Madison's heart break marriage, pg.92
2. The Owosso Angus press, Gail Russell and Madison separate, 1-12-50, pg.35
3. Kirk Crivello, Fallen Angles, 1998, pg.31
4. Macdonald Carey, Days of my life, 1991, pg.165
5. Kirk Crivello, Fallen Angles, 1998, pg.31
6. Macdonald Carey, Days of my life, 1991

Chapter 11
1. The Tuscaloosa News, Guy Madison up to pistol holsters in film work, 9-1-53, pg.37
2. Dennis Devine, Your friend, and mine: Andy Devine, 2103, pg.76
3. IBID
4. IBID
5. The Dispatch, Scandalous charges are made as John Wayne divorce trial, 10-20-53, pg.1
6. The Desert News, 10-23-53
7. Erskine Johnson, The southeast Missourian, flickers, flashes from film land, 2-6-54, pg.53
8. Reading Eagle, Gail Russell jailed for drunk driving, 11-25-53, pg.8

9. Photoplay, March, 1954, Guy Madison's hear break marriage, pg.90
10. Ottawa Citizen, his television westerns have aided Guy Madison, 9-22-53, pg.17
11. Kirk Crivello, Fallen Angles, 1998, pg.30
12. Photoplay, March, 1954, Guy Madison's hear break marriage, pg.90

\# The Desert Dispatch News reported Paramount tried to get Gail to seek psychiatric care at the Menninger Clinic, but Gail refused.

\# Discovering that Gladys was an alcoholic raises the question of did she drink during her pregnancy with Gail?
Even small amounts of alcohol may cause behavioral issues with children.

\# I made several calls to mental health institutions in Washington, no records going back that far.

Chapter 12

1. The Miami news, Star Gail Russell in Hospital, 11-4-54, pg.37
2. Eugene Register-Guard, Gail Russell Starts life again, 10-20-55
3. Sunday Herald, Gail Russell sought after tipsy arrest, 2-6-55, pg.131
4. Ocala Star Banner, Actress Gail Russell settles damage suit, 11-28-56, pg.14
5. Erskine Johnson, Park City Daily News, Hollywood Today, 10-19-55, pg.39
6. Scott Eyman, John Wayne: The life and legend, 2015, pg.283
7. Herb Fagen, Duke we're glad we knew you, 1996, pg.94
8. Robert Nott, Last of the cowboy heroes: The westerns of Randolph Scott, 2000, pg.129
9. The Pittsburg Press, Town hails Gail's return, 12-6-55, pg.87
10. Bob Thompson, Reading Eagle, Gail Russell, attributes new attitude to help from God, 10-31-55, pg.28
11. IBID

12. Robert Nott, Last of the cowboy heroes: The westerns of Randolph Scott, 2000, pg.133
13. IBID
14. Sarasota Journal, Gail credits God's help in comeback, 10-31-55, pg.9
15. Emily Beiser, The Miami News, Hard luck Gail Russell tries screen comeback, 10-20-55, pg.3
16. IBID
17. Herb Fagen, Duke we're glad we knew you, 1996, pg.94
18. IBID
19. IBID
20. IBID
21. Conversation with Ron Stephenson
Gail appeared on "Here's Hollywood TV" showcasing her art work.

Chapter 13

1. Halrod Hefferman, The Pittsburg press, Gail Russell fears turndown by fans, 7-1-56, pg.35
2. Movie Views and Reviews
3. Lydia Lane, The Miami News, The colors that count, 3-27-56, pg.20
4. Schenectady Gazette, Gail Russell arrested on drunk count, 7-5-57, pg.4
5. IBID
6. Conversation with Ron Stephenson
7. Schenectady Gazette, Gail Russell arrested on drunk count, 7-5-57, pg.4
8. The Miami News, Deputies find Gail Russell Unconscious, 8-21-57, pg.2
9. IBID
10. IBID
11. Jimmy Starr, Barefoot on a barbed wire, 2001, pg.240

12. Erskine Johnson, Times Daily, Gail Russell's private war, 10-10-57, pg. 17
13. IBID
14. IBID
15. Erskine Johnson, Times Daily, Gail Russell's private war, 10-10-57, pg. 17

Chapter 14

1. Times Daily, so they say, 9-17-57, pg.15
2. The Dispatch, 2-3-58, pg.12
3. Brian Albright, Wild beyond belief, 2008, pg.139
4. A.J Fenady, Hollywood Studio magazine Vol.16, 1983, Gail Russell by candlelight
5. IBID
6. IBID
7. IBID
8. IBID
9. IBID
10. The Sydney Morning Herald, Success sickness of stars, 2-19-61, pg.5
11. Rick DuBrow, Lodi News Sentinel, Gail Russell found in apartment, 8-28-61
12. Conversation with Roger Mobley
13. The Sydney Morning Herald, Success sickness of stars, 2-19-61, pg.5
    #in a phone conversation with Andrew J. Fenady I asked him to sum up Gail, "She was a beautiful lady, talented and tragic." He expressed surprise when I informed him about her birth name of Gale. "Like Gale Storm" he replied. Fenady wasn't too familiar with the director (Lanfield) that Gail set straight. He did know of Walter Reed who witnessed the incident. Talking about Nick Adams, he strongly

believes his death was an accident, "Nick Adams would have died with his boots on kicking."

Chapter 15

1. Jimmy Lydon, letter to author.
2. Kirk Crivello, Fallen angels, 1998, pg.35
3. IBID
4. Beverly Linet, Ladd a Hollywood tragedy, 1979, pg.243
5. Michael Munn, John Wayne: The man behind the myth, 2003, pg.110
6. Motion Picture Magazine, December, 1961, pg.66
7. Conversation with Ron Stephenson
8. Sheila Graham, The Miami News, 9-23-61, pg.15
9. Photo Magazine, March, 1956, pg.48

#Bridget Madison raised the possibility that Gail was molested as a child. Other people also believed that this occurred and setting into motion Gail's traumatic life. In another conversation we talked of her brother George being favored over Gail. Her parents may have been expecting another boy when Gail was born, said Bridget.

#Jane Fonda's character in the film "The Morning After" is supposedly based on Gail Russell. Discussing this movie with Charlie, I agree with him. Other than the fact that that Fonda played an alcoholic actress there was nothing about her portrayal to remind me of Gail.

#I hope other paintings of Gail Russell will be found. Living almost 2,500 miles from California makes it hard to track them down.

#Gail's death certificate lists 1925 as her birth year. Her brother George was the contact and handled all the funeral arrangements.

Both Charlie and Bridget believe someone was with Gail on her last day. This may be hopeful thinking in her final moments.

Index

Abbott and Costello, 141

Acquanetta, 60

Adams, Nick, 161, 188

Adler, Luther, 127

Adventures of Wild Bill Hickok, 8, 137, 142, 172

Air Cadet, 89, 141, 142, 173

Allen Lewis, 14, 22, 30, 31, 34-37, 42, 43, 48, 51, 53

Anders Merry, 60

Angel and the Badman, 57, 58, 61, 62, 85, 93, 94, 114, 132, 144, 171, 173

Arnold, Jack, 155

Bachelor's Daughter, 56

Barnett, Lewis, 12

Bates, Charlie, 19, 178

Barry, Susan, 12

Barrymore, Ethel, 118

Bennett, Hugh, 24, 25

Bergman, Ingrid, 115

Bey, Turhan, 91, 131

Boetticher, Burt, 148-152

Borzage, Frank, 118, 121

Brackett, Charlie, 22, 29-32, 34-37, 43, 162

Bridges, Lloyd, 118

Britton, Barbara, 30

Broidy, William, 143

Bruce, Virginia, 123

Burton, John Wesley, 158

Canutt, Yakima, 58

Calcutta, 114, 115, 116, 117, 123, 155, 173

Calhoun, Rory, 136

Captain China, 133, 134, 173

Carey, Harry, 58, 80

Carey, Harry Jr., 126

Carey, Macdonald, 138-140

Carson, Jack, 155, 156

Castle, Peggie, 142

Chaplin, Charlie, 12

Chandler, Jeff, 155, 156

Chandler, Raymond, 48, 51, 52, 123

Chase, Charles, 19, 178

Clark, Dane, 10, 118

Coleman, Herbert, 115, 116

Columbia Pictures, 130

Connolly, Shelia, 146

Cooper, Gary, 46, 115

Crain, Jeanne, 155, 156

Crisp, Donald, 33, 35

Crosby, Bing, 23, 46

Crowther, Brosley, 47, 126

Curtis, Tony, 141

Dan Patch, 133

Darrell, Virginia, 9, 10

Davis, Bette, 55

De Carlo, Yvonne, 44

Demarest, William, 123

DeMille, Cecil, 48, 115

DeSylva, Buddy, 22, 29, 32, 43

Deutsch, Leonard, 148

Devine, Andy, 8, 142, 143, 171, 175, 185

Dillinger, Bert, 145

Edison, Thomas, 22

Edouart, Farciot, 30

Eden, Barbara, 116

Egil, Joe, 33

El Paso, 96, 132, 154, 173

Emma, Ruth, 8, 12, 68, 180

Fairbanks, Douglas, 33, 46

Farrow, John, 114-117, 123-126, 128

Farrow, Mia, 114, 116, 182

Fenady, J. Andrew, 5, 162, 161, 163, 187

Fix, Paul, 128, 127

Foppiano, Kathrine, 9

Frank, W.K., 133

Freed, Arthur, 60

Gardner, Ava, 39, 141

Garfield, John, 118, 175, 183

Gershwin, Ira, 26

Grant, James, 58, 61

Grant, Marshall, 118

Griffin, D.W., 33, 46

Griffin, Nona, 74, 86, 99

Haas, Charles, 118

Hayden Sterling, 141

Head, Edith, 52

Henaghan, Jim, 169

Henry Aldrich Gets Glamour, 24-26, 44, 106, 173

Hill, Howard, 134

Hitchcock, Alfred, 29, 115

Hope, Bob, 31, 46

Houseman, John, 48, 51, 52

Hudson, Rock, 142

Hunter, Tab, 125, 174, 183

Hussey, Ruth, 33, 34, 35, 37, 39, 40

Ingram, Rex, 118, 122

Joslyn, Allyn, 118, 121

Johnson, Erskine, 158

Keaton, Buster, 33

Kennedy, Burt, 149

King, Joyce, 160

Kimbrough, Emily, 43-45

Kline, C. Leo, 168

Ladd, Alan, 10, 23, 46, 47, 61, 114, 115, 168

Lady in the Dark, 26-28, 132, 154, 173

Lamarr, Hedy, 19

Lamour, Dorothy, 33, 44, 46

Lanfield, Sidney, 31, 47, 57

Lang, Charles, 30, 34

Lasky, Jesse, 22

Lawford, Peter, 114

Lawless, The, 137, 138, 173

Lawrence, Catalina, 58

Lava, William, 118

Leisen, Mitchell, 26-29

Lewis, Milton, 19, 21, 168, 169

Lloyd, Norman, 49, 52

Lockhart, June, 30-32, 166, 180

Long, Richard, 142

Lopez, Carmelita, 42

Losey, Joseph, 137, 138

Lund, John, 89, 97, 123, 124

Lydon, Jimmy, 5, 23-26, 61, 168, 188

Lynn, Diana, 25, 43, 44, 55, 60, 168

Macardle, Dorothy, 28, 29

Madison, Guy, 8, 10, 54, 62, 67, 112-114, 129, 130, 133-137, 142-147, 161, 171, 172

Manhunt, 165

Manly, Nellie, 162

Mara, Adele, 127, 128

Marshall, Herbert, 48, 49, 52

Marvin, Lee, 97, 152 153

Mayer, L.B, 60, 61

McCrea, Joel, 48, 52

McLeod, Catherine, 126

McNally, Steve, 141, 142

Meiklejohn, William, 19, 20, 31, 178

Milland, Ray, 32-35, 37, 39, 61, 96

Mitchell, Johnny, 114

Mitchum, Robert, 116, 125, 149, 175, 183

Mobley, Roger, 5, 98, 166, 167

Monahan, Detective, 9

Moonrise, 10, 92, 99, 100, 114, 118, 122-124

Morgan, Henry, 118, 121

Moseley, Mrs., 9

Napier, Alan, 33

Night has a Thousand Eyes, 123, 124, 126, 173

No Place to Land, 160

O'Hara, Dorothy, 52

Our Hearts Were Young and Gay, 43-46, 54, 55

O'Sullivan, Maureen, 114, 125

Paramount Studios, 19-26, 29, 31, 33, 35, 37, 40-44, 48, 59, 60, 61, 114, 115, 117, 131-136, 138, 140, 162, 168, 175,

Payne, John, 87, 96, 132-134

Parson, Louella, 53, 54, 178, 181

Poe, Allen Edgar, 53, 123

Rebel, the, 161, 162, 165, 173

Reed, Walter, 31, 153

Reichman, Jerry, 157

Republic Studios, 57, 58, 118, 122, 123, 126-128

Reynolds, Roberts, 157

Robinson, G. Edward, 89, 97, 123, 124, 126

Rodgers, Ginger, 16, 26-28

Rodgers, Dale, Roy, 159

Russell, Gale Betty, 11, 13, 66, 171, 178

Russell, Elizabeth, 34, 40

Russell, Jane, 18, 33, 159

Russell, George Sr., 11-16, 18-20, 68, 151, 160, 170

Russell, George Jr., 11, 15, 18, 20, 47, 68, 171

Russell, Barnett, Gladys, 8, 11-15, 18, 20, 21, 53, 74, 151, 158, 170

Russell, Samuel, 12

Russell, William, 22, 24, 25, 27, 31, 35, 43, 54, 168, 171

Sabu, 91, 131

Salty O'Rourke, 46, 47, 98

Santa Monica Tech, 19, 178

Seitz, Johnny, 116, 124

Seven Men from Now, 148, 149-154, 173

Scott, Lizabeth, 87, 125

Scott, Randolph, 149, 150

Shay, Dorothy, 156, 159

Skinner Otis Cornelia, 33, 42-46

Stanwyck, Barbara, 125, 175

Stella, Mary, 8, 68, 69, 71, 101

Stephenson, Ron, 5, 55, 153, 157, 169

Stewart, Elaine, 155

St. John, Mary, 57, 62

Stout, Archie, 58, 64

Strauss, Theodore, 118

Sturges, Preston, 30

Sullivan, Eddie, 115

Smith, Dodie, 29-32

Song of India, 130, 131

Swanson, Gloria, 12

Sweeney, Ed, 145

Tattered Dress, The, 88, 155, 173

Taylor, Elizabeth, 59

Timmons, Charlie, 5, 8, 12, 158, 168

Todd, Thelma, 61, 174

Totter, Audrey, 60

Turner, Lana, 125

Trevor, Claire, 56

Uninvited, The, 6, 8, 114, 29, 30, 31, 33, 34, 35, 37-43, 47, 48, 51-53, 64, 89, 96, 116, 130, 162, 163, 173

University High School, 18, 76, 77

Unseen, The, 6, 48, 51-53, 86, 90, 99, 122, 171, 173

Van Nuys High School, 18

Variety Girl, 117

Wake of the Red Witch, 6, 94, 95, 126, 128, 130, 132, 134, 171, 173

Walker, Helen, 30, 32, 44

Walsh, Raoul, 46

Warner Brothers, 123, 148, 153

Wayne, John (The Duke), 6, 10, 17, 21, 46, 57, 58, 59, 61, 62, 64, 77, 114, 125-130, 143, 144, 148, 153, 163, 168, 171

Wayne, Chata, 61, 62, 144

Weatherwax, Rudd, 34, 166

Weill, Kurt, 26

Weissmuller, Johnny, 114

West, Yvonne, 148

Westmore, Wally, 162

White, Lina Ethel, 47

Wild, Hagar, 52

Wilder, Billy, 29-32

Wilson Junior High School, 17

Woolrich, Cornell, 123

Young, Gig, 127, 128

Young, Victor, 36

Zukor, Adolph, 21, 22, 23

www.ingramcontent.com/pod-product-compliance
Lightning Source LLC
Chambersburg PA
CBHW071918290426
44110CB00013B/1408